Sexual Violence

Other Books of Related Interest:

Opposing Viewpoints Series

Feminism

Online Pornography

At Issue Series

Date Rape

Current Controversies

Violence Against Women

"Congress shall make
no law . . . abridging
the freedom of speech,
or of the press."

First Amendment to the U.S. Constitution

The basic foundation of our democracy is the First Amendment guarantee of freedom of expression. The Opposing Viewpoints Series is dedicated to the concept of this basic freedom and the idea that it is more important to practice it than to enshrine it.

OPPOSING VIEWPOINTS® SERIES

Sexual Violence

Louise I. Gerdes, Book Editor

GREENHAVEN PRESS
A part of Gale, Cengage Learning

Detroit • New York • San Francisco • New Haven, Conn • Waterville, Maine • London

Christine Nasso, *Publisher*
Elizabeth Des Chenes, *Managing Editor*

© 2008 Greenhaven Press, a part of Gale, Cengage Learning

Gale and Greenhaven Press are registered trademarks used herein under license.

For more information, contact:
Greenhaven Press
27500 Drake Rd.
Farmington Hills, MI 48331-3535
Or you can visit our Internet site at gale.cengage.com

For product information and technology assistance, contact us at

Gale Customer Support, 1-800-877-4253
For permission to use material from this text or product, submit all requests online at www.cengage.com/permissions

Further permissions questions can be emailed to permissionrequest@cengage.com

Articles in Greenhaven Press anthologies are often edited for length to meet page requirements. In addition, original titles of these works are changed to clearly present the main thesis and to explicitly indicate the author's opinion. Every effort is made to ensure that Greenhaven Press accurately reflects the original intent of the authors. Every effort has been made to trace the owners of copyrighted material.

Cover photograph © Yellow Dog Productions/Stone/Getty Images

LIBRARY OF CONGRESS CATALOGING-IN-PUBLICATION DATA

Sexual violence / Louise I. Gerdes, book editor.
    p. cm. -- (Opposing viewpoints)
    Includes bibliographical references and index.
    ISBN-13: 978-0-7377-4010-3 (hardcover)
    ISBN-13: 978-0-7377-4011-0 (pbk.)
    1. Sex crimes--United States. 2. Rape--United States. 3. Sex offenders--United States.
I. Gerdes, Louise I., 1953-
    HV6592.S4865 2008
    364.15'3--dc22

                                                                2008008133

Printed in the United States of America
1 2 3 4 5 6 7 12 11 10 09 08

Contents

Chapter 2: What Factors Contribute to Sexual Violence?

Chapter 3: How Should Society Respond to Sexual Violence?

Chapter 4: What Policies Will Help Reduce Sexual Violence?

Why Consider
Opposing Viewpoints?

> *"The only way in which a human being can make some approach to knowing the whole of a subject is by hearing what can be said about it by persons of every variety of opinion and studying all modes in which it can be looked at by every character of mind. No wise man ever acquired his wisdom in any mode but this."*
>
> *John Stuart Mill*

In our media-intensive culture it is not difficult to find differing opinions. Thousands of newspapers and magazines and dozens of radio and television talk shows resound with differing points of view. The difficulty lies in deciding which opinion to agree with and which "experts" seem the most credible. The more inundated we become with differing opinions and claims, the more essential it is to hone critical reading and thinking skills to evaluate these ideas. Opposing Viewpoints books address this problem directly by presenting stimulating debates that can be used to enhance and teach these skills. The varied opinions contained in each book examine many different aspects of a single issue. While examining these conveniently edited opposing views, readers can develop critical thinking skills such as the ability to compare and contrast authors' credibility, facts, argumentation styles, use of persuasive techniques, and other stylistic tools. In short, the Opposing Viewpoints Series is an ideal way to attain the higher-level thinking and reading skills so essential in a culture of diverse and contradictory opinions.

In addition to providing a tool for critical thinking, Opposing Viewpoints books challenge readers to question their own strongly held opinions and assumptions. Most people form their opinions on the basis of upbringing, peer pressure, and personal, cultural, or professional bias. By reading carefully balanced opposing views, readers must directly confront new ideas as well as the opinions of those with whom they disagree. This is not to simplistically argue that everyone who reads opposing views will—or should—change his or her opinion. Instead, the series enhances readers' understanding of their own views by encouraging confrontation with opposing ideas. Careful examination of others' views can lead to the readers' understanding of the logical inconsistencies in their own opinions, perspective on why they hold an opinion, and the consideration of the possibility that their opinion requires further evaluation.

Evaluating Other Opinions

To ensure that this type of examination occurs, Opposing Viewpoints books present all types of opinions. Prominent spokespeople on different sides of each issue as well as well-known professionals from many disciplines challenge the reader. An additional goal of the series is to provide a forum for other, less known, or even unpopular viewpoints. The opinion of an ordinary person who has had to make the decision to cut off life support from a terminally ill relative, for example, may be just as valuable and provide just as much insight as a medical ethicist's professional opinion. The editors have two additional purposes in including these less known views. One, the editors encourage readers to respect others' opinions—even when not enhanced by professional credibility. It is only by reading or listening to and objectively evaluating others' ideas that one can determine whether they are worthy of consideration. Two, the inclusion of such viewpoints encourages the important critical thinking skill of objectively evaluating an author's credentials and bias. This evaluation will illuminate an author's reasons for taking a particular stance on an issue and will aid in readers' evaluation of the author's ideas.

It is our hope that these books will give readers a deeper understanding of the issues debated and an appreciation of the complexity of even seemingly simple issues when good and honest people disagree. This awareness is particularly important in a democratic society such as ours in which people enter into public debate to determine the common good. Those with whom one disagrees should not be regarded as enemies but rather as people whose views deserve careful examination and may shed light on one's own.

Thomas Jefferson once said that "difference of opinion leads to inquiry, and inquiry to truth." Jefferson, a broadly educated man, argued that "if a nation expects to be ignorant and free . . . it expects what never was and never will be." As individuals and as a nation, it is imperative that we consider the opinions of others and examine them with skill and discernment. The Opposing Viewpoints Series is intended to help readers achieve this goal.

David L. Bender and Bruno Leone,
Founders

Introduction

> "Laws defining and setting punishments for rape have varied enormously among different cultures and during different time periods. Throughout history, rape laws have illustrated a culture's social and political attitudes about sex and gender."—Susan N. Herman, professor of law, Brooklyn Law School.

Although sexual assault is one of the most rapidly growing violent crimes in America, many call it a silent epidemic. Indeed, U.S. Department of Justice statistics suggest that rape, the most common form of sexual assault, is the most under-reported crime. According to the American Medical Association (AMA), "Less than half of rapes are reported to authorities." Over the years, analysts have suggested many reasons why victims do not always report rape. AMA president Lonnie Bristow contends, "This crime is shrouded in silence, caused by unfair social myths and biases that incriminate victims rather than offenders. These myths push victims into the shadows, afraid to step forward and seek help." Research does in fact show that some victims believe that they have not been raped if they do not physically resist. Other victims think that it is not rape if they are sexually assaulted by an acquaintance or family member. Many of these mistaken beliefs about rape do have a foundation in older rape laws. As the result of research and activism, however, rape law has evolved. How the law defines rape does indeed reflect shifting cultural attitudes toward both the victims and the perpetrators of sexual violence.

Both the United States and Canada modeled their laws on English common law, which defined rape as the sexual penetration of a woman forcibly and against her will. Until recent decades, the common law rules of evidence were designed not to punish offenders, but to protect men from false accusations. For example, the "utmost resistance doctrine" provided that a man could only be convicted if his victim demonstrated that she had attempted to fight off the rape. According to the "fresh complaint rule" a case could only be heard if a woman promptly reported the rape. Rape convictions were made even more difficult in the United States. In addition to these common law rules, U.S. law required corroborating physical evidence of forcible rape such as semen, bruises, or witness testimony—evidence that was often difficult to obtain.

In the 1960s, activists challenged the assumption that the accused needed more protection than the rape victim. Women's groups protested that the utmost resistance doctrine unfairly forced rape victims to risk death or serious injury in order to convict rapists. Rape research also revealed that the traumatic impact of rape made it difficult for many victims to report rape to the authorities. In 1972 Ann Wolbert Burgess and Lynda Lytle Holstrom interviewed and counseled rape victims at a Boston hospital. They identified a pattern of reactions to rape that they called Rape Trauma Syndrome. The response to rape, they assert, may be so severe that victims will not reveal their ordeal to friends or family and may not seek help from the police. Rape law activists argued that this research called into question the fairness of the fresh complaint rule, as many victims might not acknowledge that they had been raped until days, weeks, months, or even years after the rape. Because of new attitudes and understanding about rape, in the 1970s most states began to change their laws by redefining rape and eliminating some of the common law doctrines and biases against victims.

Another legal development that reflects changing cultural attitudes toward rape is a shifting definition of what constitutes nonconsensual sex. Although most jurisdictions have removed the physical force requirement and define rape as sexual intercourse without valid consent, "some victims of attacks meeting the legal definition of rape do not label their experience as sexual assault," the AMA explains. Some believe, for example, that people cannot be raped by someone they know. As sociologists and psychologists began to study rape, however, they discovered that the most commonly recognized form of rape, stranger rape, is in fact the least commonly perpetrated. Only about 20 percent of sexual assaults against women are perpetrated by strangers. The majority of rapes in the United States are what is known as acquaintance or date rapes, in which the victim knows the attacker. Not until the 1980s, however, did the public acknowledge the problem of acquaintance rape. While rape law never required that the victim and perpetrator be strangers, it did require that the sex be nonconsensual. The controversy surrounding acquaintance rape remains heated not because of the relationship between the victim and the perpetrator but because in cases of alleged acquaintance rape the issue of consent can be less clear.

Those who see acquaintance rape as a serious problem argue that nonconsensual sex should be defined broadly. Even if subtle, they claim, coercion removes consent from the sexual act and is therefore rape. According to psychology professors Julie A. Allison and Lawrence S. Wrightsman, "A rape is a rape and its consequences cannot be trivialized just because of some prior expectations by the woman or prior relationships with the assailant." Those who support a broad definition of nonconsensual sex assert that the coercion in an acquaintance rape can be as overt as holding the victim down or twisting her arm or as subtle as verbal abuse and threats. Some observers see verbal manipulation as a form of coercion. Some acquaintance rapists, they maintain, suggest that refusing to have sex will change the way the assailant sees the victim while others may threaten to end the relationship. "Even though victims may not label the experience as rape per se,"

Allison and Wrightsman note, "they suffer similar psychological and physical consequences as those self-acknowledged rape victims."

Opponents of broad definitions fear that if consent is defined from the victim's point of view, an accused who honestly believed that consent had been given might be unjustly punished. Determining consent, these commentators claim, is highly subjective and influenced by varying attitudes toward gender, sexuality, and individual responsibility. Moreover, some argue that equating verbal manipulation with physical coercion trivializes the problem of sexual violence. "There still remains a world of difference between a smooth talker on the one hand and a man holding a knife to your throat on the other. Calling them both rapists may be a fine way of highlighting the malignity of the former, but it is also a way of trivializing the criminality of the latter," maintains David R. Carlin, who writes for the conservative Catholic magazine, *Commonweal*.

In an effort to protect rape victims as well as those falsely accused of rape, lawmakers continue to struggle with how to define nonconsensual sex. Whether modern developments in the law of rape have given too much protection to victims and too little to those accused of rape, or whether such developments are necessary to encourage victims to report rape and bring rapists to justice, remains controversial. The authors of the viewpoints in *Opposing Viewpoints: Sexual Violence* explore other issues concerning the nature and scope of sexual violence in the following chapters: Is Sexual Violence a Serious Problem? What Factors Contribute to Sexual Violence? How Should Society Respond to Sexual Violence? What Policies Will Help Reduce Sexual Violence?

CHAPTER 1

Is Sexual Violence a Serious Problem?

Chapter Preface

After Texas prison officials repeatedly ignored his complaints of rape and sexual abuse, seventeen-year-old Rodney Hulin hanged himself with a sheet in 1996. Prison-rape activists maintain that the sexual abuse Hulin experienced is a common problem faced by prisoners nationwide. Unfortunately, while rape outside prison is considered a horrific crime, they argue, rape in prison is considered a joke, an acceptable source of humor in popular culture. Even among those who do not believe prison rape is a joke, some have little sympathy for the victims, believing that prison rape is inevitable, part of the price of committing crimes. Indeed, one of several debates concerning the scope of the problem of sexual violence is whether prison rape is a serious problem that must be addressed.

According to prison rape activists, the problem of prison rape is a serious threat to prisoners and the community. A study conducted by psychology professor Cindy Struckman-Johnson and colleagues found that "22 to 25% of prisoners are the victims of sexual pressuring, attempted sexual assault, or completed rapes." At least one in ten prisoners in the study claimed to have been the victim of rape at least once while incarcerated. Because victims are incarcerated, prison rape is often more devastating to the victim than for those outside, mental health counselor Robert W. Dumond maintains. Prison rape is more likely to be accompanied by physical abuse and to occur repeatedly due to the nature of incarceration. As a result, "most victims are at risk of committing suicide as a means of avoiding the ongoing trauma," he claims. Prison rape also threatens public health. "Victims may contract HIV/AIDS, other sexually transmitted diseases, [and] other communicable diseases," Dumond explains. "These diseases can be spread to others in both the prison population and the general community," he asserts. Unfortunately, surveys reveal that most correctional officials deny that prison rape is a problem. "Criminal prosecution," Dumond observes, "is virtually non-existent in cases of prisoner sexual assault."

While most observers agree that prison rape is a terrible crime, those who oppose spending tax dollars on programs to study and reduce prison rape claim that the problem is exaggerated. Indeed, study estimates vary substantially. Gerald G. Gaes of the Federal Bureau of Prisons and Andrew L. Goldberg of the National Institute of Justice found that "estimates of how many male inmates experience forced sex during incarcerations range from nearly 10 percent to less than 1 percent." Libertarian writer Cathy Young cautions that it would be unwise "to accept the activists' claims at face value. As we have learned from the examples of domestic violence, sexual assault on campus, and homelessness, advocacy groups are prone to the abuse of statistics—and to the use of unreliable narratives." A controversial critic of the claim that prison rape is widespread is cultural anthropologist Mark S. Fleisher. His May 2006 study "The Culture of Prison Sexual Violence" asserts that the media perpetuate the myth that sexual violence in prison is widespread. He claims that most inmates see the sexual activity in prison as consensual. Fleisher reports that many prisoners believe that "a man cannot be raped unless he wants to be."

The scope of the problem of prison rape remains controversial. The authors in the following chapter debate other controversies surrounding the scope of sexual violence.

> *"All forms of sexual violence harm the individual, the family unit, and society."*

Rape and Sexual Violence Are Serious Problems

National Institute of Justice

Sexual violence continues to be a serious social problem, claims the National Institute of Justice (NIJ) in the following viewpoint. Despite campaigns to increase awareness and protect victims, the authors maintain, a majority of rape victims still fear reporting assaults, particularly if the victim knows the perpetrator. Unfortunately, a majority of sexual assaults are committed by people known to the victim, the NIJ asserts. Indeed, studies that report lower rape rates exclude such assaults, the authors note. The NIJ is a research agency of the U.S. Department of Justice.

As you read, consider the following questions:

1. According to the NIJ, what are some of the unwanted behaviors included in the definition of sexual assault?

2. What are some of the reasons why victims may not report sexual assault, in the authors' view?

National Institute of Justice, "Rape and Sexual Violence," *U.S. Department of Justice.* www.ojp.usdoj.gov/nij.

3. Who is more likely to be injured during a sexual assault, in the authors' opinion, men or women?

The term "sexual violence" refers to a specific constellation of crimes including sexual harassment, sexual assault, and rape. The perpetrator may be a stranger, acquaintance, friend, family member, or intimate partner. Researchers, practitioners, and policymakers agree that all forms of sexual violence harm the individual, the family unit, and society and that much work remains to be done to enhance the criminal justice response to these crimes.

Sexual Violence Takes Many Forms

Sexual harassment ranges from degrading remarks, gestures, and jokes to indecent exposure, being touched, grabbed, pinched, or brushed against in a sexual way. In employment settings, it has been defined as "unwelcome sexual advances, requests for sexual favors, and other verbal or physical conduct that enters into employment decisions or conduct that unreasonably interferes with an individual's work performance or creates an intimidating, hostile, or offensive working environment."

Sexual assault covers a wide range of unwanted behaviors—up to but not including penetration—that are attempted or completed against a victim's will or when a victim cannot consent because of age, disability, or the influence of alcohol or drugs. Sexual assault may involve actual or threatened physical force, use of weapons, coercion, intimidation, or pressure and may include—

- Intentional touching of the victim's genitals, anus, groin, or breasts.

- Voyeurism.

- Exposure to exhibitionism.

- Undesired exposure to pornography.

- Public display of images that were taken in a private context or when the victim was unaware.

Rape definitions vary by State and in response to legislative advocacy. Most statutes currently define rape as nonconsensual oral, anal, or vaginal penetration of the victim by body parts or objects using force, threats of bodily harm, or by taking advantage of a victim who is incapacitated or otherwise incapable of giving consent. Incapacitation may include mental or cognitive disability, self-induced or forced intoxication, status as minor, or any other condition defined by law that voids an individual's ability to give consent.

Not surprisingly, rates of rape also vary widely among studies according to how the crime is defined, what population is studied, and what methodology is used. Estimates range from as low as 2 percent to 56 percent. The most recent and methodologically rigorous studies show that sexual assault still occurs at rates that approximate those first identified more than 20 years ago when [M.P.] Koss, [C.A.] Gidycz, and [N.] Wisiewski, 1987, reported that approximately 27.5 percent of college women reported experiences that met the legal criteria for rape.

Sexual assault and rape are generally defined as felonies. During the past 30 years, States have enacted rape shield laws to protect victims and criminal and civil legal remedies to punish perpetrators. The effectiveness of these laws in accomplishing their goals is a topic of concern.

Estimates also vary regarding how likely a victim is to report her victimization. Traditionally, rape notification rates differed depending on whether the victim knew the perpetrator—those who knew a perpetrator were often less likely to report the crime. This gap, however, may be closing.

Are Rape Notification Rates Increasing?

Does the victim-offender relationship remain an important predictor of the likelihood of police notification in rape cases?

An NIJ-funded study examined this question and found that police notification rates by third parties and by victims who had been raped by an acquaintance or intimate partner increased significantly between 1973 and 2000. Using data from the National Crime Survey (NCS) from 1973–1991 and the National Crime Victimization Survey (NCVS) from 1992–2000, [E.P.] Baumer found that overall reporting rates continued to increase during the 1990s, and that differences in rates of reporting between stranger and non-stranger rapes diminished.

These changes coincided with large-scale media and social campaigns that focused attention on "hidden" rapes. Legal reforms and the growth in services available to rape victims have been influential in increasing the likelihood that women will report a rape to police.

The most recent research, however, indicates that a majority of rape victims still do not report their attacks to police. Further study is needed to understand what impact various policies and practices have on reporting behavior and system response and to precisely identify the practices that would facilitate higher rates of notification.

Victims and Perpetrators

Research on sexual violence indicates that—

Sexual violence may occur in any type of relationship, but most perpetrators of sexual assault are known to their victims. Among victims ages 18 to 29, two-thirds had a prior relationship with the offender. The Bureau of Justice Statistics (BJS) reports that, in 2000, 6 in 10 rape or sexual assault victims said that they were assaulted by an intimate partner, relative, friend, or acquaintance. A study of sexual victimization of college women showed that 9 out of 10 victims knew the person who sexually victimized them. One research project found that 34 percent of women surveyed were victims of sexual coercion by a husband or intimate partner in their lifetime.

Most Victims Know Their Attacker

The vast majority of sexual-assault victims are attacked by family members or acquaintances, not strangers.

Offenders (by percentage)

Victim Age	Family member	Acquaintance	Stranger
All victims	26.7%	59.6%	13.8%
Juveniles	34.2	58.7	7.0
0–5 years old	48.6	48.3	3.1
6–11	42.4	52.9	4.7
12–17	24.3	66.0	9.8
Adults			
18–24	9.8	66.5	23.7
24+	12.8	57.1	30.1

TAKEN FROM: "Sexual Assault of Young Children as Reported to Law Enforcement: Victim, Incident, and Offender Characteristics," Bureau of Justice Statistics, U.S. Department of Justice, July 2000.

The majority of sexual assaults are not reported to the authorities. BJS reports that the majority of rapes and sexual assaults perpetrated against women and girls in the United States between 1992 and 2000 were not reported to the police. Only 36 percent of rapes, 34 percent of attempted rapes, and 26 percent of sexual assaults were reported. Reasons for not reporting assault vary among individuals, but [J.] Du Mont, [K.L.] Miller and [I.L.] Myhr, 2003, identified the following as common:

- Self-blame or guilt.

- Shame, embarrassment, or desire to keep the assault a private matter.

- Humiliation or fear of the perpetrator or other individual's perceptions.

- Fear of not being believed or of being accused of playing a role in the crime.

• Lack of trust in the criminal justice system.

Women are more likely to be victims of sexual violence than are men. The National Violence Against Women (NVAW) Survey sampled 8,000 women and 8,000 men and found that 1 in 6 women (17 percent) and 1 in 33 men (3 percent) reported experiencing an attempted or completed rape at some time in their lives.

Sexual violence may begin early in life. Researchers also found that among female rape victims surveyed, more than half (54 percent) were younger than age 18; 32.4 percent were ages 12–17; and 21.6 percent were younger than age 12 at time of victimization.

Studying Sexual Violence

Sexual assault and injury. Women are significantly more likely than men to be injured during an assault in one NIJ-funded study, 31.5 percent of female rape victims, compared with 16.1 percent of male rape victims, reported being injured during their most recent rape.

Assault among college women. A survey of college women found that 2.8 percent had experienced either a completed (1.7 percent) or an attempted (1.1 percent) rape within a 9-month timeframe. This rate is approximately 11 times higher than the rate found using a survey that is specifically crime oriented, such as the NCVS.

Sexual assault in intimate partner relationships. The few studies that measure sexual assault separately from physical assault within intimate partner relationships report that 40 to 50 percent of battered women are also sexually assaulted by their partners. In another study, researchers found that 68 percent of physically abused women reported that their partners sexually assaulted them.

Early abuse and later victimization. Although child sexual abuse before age 13 is not by itself a risk factor for adult sexual victimization or domestic violence, girls who were victimized before turning 12 and then again as adolescents (ages 13–17) were at much greater risk of both types of victimization as adults than any other women.

Effective responses to sexual assault. An NIJ impact evaluation, [by C.S.] Crandall and [D.] Helitzer, 2003, found that Sexual Assault Nurse Examiner (SANE) programs and multidisciplinary Sexual Assault Response Teams (SART):

- Enhance the quality of health care for women who have been sexually assaulted.

- Improve the quality of forensic evidence.

- Increase law enforcement's ability to collect information, file charges, and prosecute and convict the assailant.

According to the International Association of Forensic Nurses, at least 276 SANE programs operate throughout the United States and its territories, most based in hospitals (75 percent), but some located in community settings (25 percent).

Rape and sexual assault in prison. NIJ has sponsored several studies concerning rape and sexual assault within correctional facilities, including studies that look at prevalence, inmate and staff perceptions, and how State and local correctional facilities are complying with the Prison Rape Elimination Act of 2003.

| *"Rape in America is receding, and rap-idly."*

Rape and Sexual Violence Appear to Be Declining

David A. Fahrenthold

Since the 1970s, there appears to have been a substantial reduction in sexual violence in America, asserts David A. Fahrenthold in the following viewpoint. While some attribute the decline to a shrinking youth population and the abatement of the crack cocaine epidemic, he notes, others argue that women have learned to better protect themselves and that both sexes better understand the rules of sexual consent. While rape remains an underreported crime, decades of efforts to protect victims have increased the reporting of rapes and sexual assaults, making the decline surprising for many, while others remain dubious, the author maintains. Fahrenthold is a Washington Post *staff writer.*

As you read, consider the following questions:

1. In Fahrenthold's opinion, why do some claim that the declining number of rapes may be a statistical mirage?
2. What efforts and policies have increased rape reporting, in the author's view?

3. According to the author, what are some of the measures used to track the decline in rape?

The number of rapes per capita in the United States has plunged by more than 85 percent since the 1970s, and reported rape fell [in 2005] even while other violent offenses increased, according to federal crime data.

This seemingly stunning reduction in sexual violence has been so consistent over the past two decades that some experts say they have started to believe it is accurate, even if they cannot fully explain why it is occurring.

In 1979, according to a Justice Department estimate based on a wide-ranging public survey, there were 2.8 rapes for every 1,000 people. In 2004, the same survey found that the rate had decreased to 0.4 per thousand.

Looking for Answers

Many criminologists and victims' advocates say that these numbers could be a statistical mirage, because rape is still underreported and poorly understood. But others say they have been convinced that there is real improvement and that a devastating crime has been receding from American life.

"Overall, there has clearly been a decline over the last 10 to 20 years," said Kim Gandy, president of the National Organization for Women. "It's very liberating for women, in terms of now being able to be more free and more safe."

By all accounts, rape is still one of the most underreported crimes. Several decades after the establishment of rape crisis hotlines, greater sensitivity toward rape victims by police and prosecutors, adoption of policies by news organizations to not identify victims and limitations on how much a victim's sexual history can be placed in evidence during trial, the Justice Department estimates that 61 percent of rapes and sexual assaults are still not reported. But that is down from 69 percent in 1996, and experts say the trend remains downward.

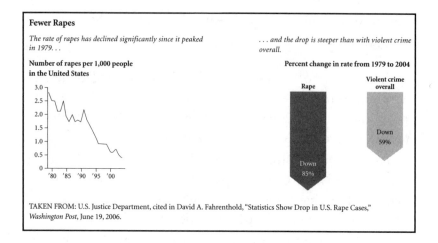

Fewer Rapes

The rate of rapes has declined significantly since it peaked in 1979...

...and the drop is steeper than with violent crime overall.

Number of rapes per 1,000 people in the United States

Percent change in rate from 1979 to 2004

TAKEN FROM: U.S. Justice Department, cited in David A. Fahrenthold, "Statistics Show Drop in U.S. Rape Cases," *Washington Post,* June 19, 2006.

Not everyone is convinced that things are getting that much better. Many who work with rape victims say they do not believe there has been a widespread decline in the number of attacks. Instead—despite the years of attempted outreach to rape victims—they say the crime may be as hidden now as ever.

"If there's been a change, it's been a very small change," said Dean Kilpatrick, director of the National Crime Victims Research and Treatment Center in Charleston, S.C. He said that recent high-profile rape cases such as those involving Duke University lacrosse players and basketball star Kobe Bryant may have persuaded rape victims to stay silent because of public scrutiny of the accusers' private lives and sexual history.

Some experts say that the dispute over numbers has made rape an especially difficult crime to study or try to fix.

"When the conversation gets bogged down around, 'How prevalent is this problem?' you can't even get to the next steps, of 'Now, what are we going to do about it?'" said Jennifer Pollitt Hill, executive director of the Maryland Coalition Against Sexual Assault, an Arnold-based umbrella group for victims' assistance groups statewide.

Tracking Rape's Decline

Now, though, some experts are saying they have been won over by decades of data showing the same encouraging thing: Rape in America is receding, and rapidly.

One measure is the Justice Department's National Crime Victimization Survey, which asks thousands of respondents 12 and older about crimes that have happened to them. This survey, which is meant to capture offenses that weren't reported to police, is the one that depicted the 85 percent decline in the per-capita rape rate since 1979.

Another way to track rape's apparent decline is through the nation's police reports, which are aggregated every year by the FBI. Their reports, dating to the mid-1980s, show that rape reached a peak in about 1992, with 0.4 rapes reported to police per 1,000 people.

Since then, reported rape declined about 25 percent by 2004, the most recent year for which data were available. In that year, the rate was about 0.3 reported rapes per 1,000. Besides the fact that not all rapes were being reported, the two studies' differ because the FBI reports define rape more narrowly, excluding instances involving male victims. Both classify attempted rapes as "rape."

[In June 2006] the FBI released its preliminary crime data for 2005, which showed that reports of rape had again fallen slightly—even as other violent crimes such as murder and robbery ticked worrisomely upward.

"The decline has been steady and consistent, which gives us a lot of confidence that it's a real occurrence, not a statistical anomaly," said Scott Berkowitz, president of the Washington-based Rape, Abuse and Incest National Network.

Explaining the Decline

One school of thought holds that rape has declined for the same reasons that other violent offenses have: a reduction in the lawlessness associated with crack cocaine, a shrinking population of young people and an increased number of criminals in jail.

Rapists "tend to commit other crimes," said Richard Felson, a professor at Pennsylvania State University. "The way we say it in criminology is that offenders tend to be versatile." By this logic, locking up robbers, killers and drug dealers reduces the pool of potential rapists out on the street.

Another, more hopeful, explanation is that Americans have actually changed the way they think about sexual assault: Women have been taught to avoid unsafe situations, and both boys and girls have been drilled to understand the rules of consent.

"They're far more aware that 'no' means no," than previous generations, Berkowitz said.

In the Washington area . . . local officials said they had seen little evidence of a vast decline in rape. [In 2005] the District's total rapes fell 24 percent; at the same time, reports of rape increased in several suburban jurisdictions.

Because the recent federal report on crime statistics counts only cities, statistics on other local jurisdictions were not included.

"I think we're steady in Prince George's County," said [Maryland] State's Attorney Glenn F. Ivey. He said county authorities have seen new and disturbing trends in sexual assault, including a spate of attacks by juveniles and a few assaults committed at school-day "skip parties." Ivey recalled one recent skip party at which a girl was allegedly surprised and attacked by eight or nine men as a kind of gang initiation.

"I just don't recall seeing things like that 10 or 15 years ago," Ivey said.

> *"Thirty percent of female veterans . . . reported rape or attempted rape during active duty."*

Sexual Violence Is a Serious Problem for Women in the Military

Jane Hoppen

Nearly one-third of women in the military report that they have been sexually assaulted while on active duty, asserts feminist writer Jane Hoppen in the following viewpoint. Many of these women must continue to take orders from their attackers, increasing their feelings of helplessness, she claims. Nevertheless, Hoppen contends, the military continues to cover up the problem, and often further adds to the victims' trauma by asking them to remain silent. The Department of Defense has taken some steps to address the situation, but the author points out that, in the past, the military's efforts to prevent sexual assault have not led to significant change.

Jane Hoppen, "Women in the Military: Who's Got Your Back?" *off our backs*, vol. 36, 2006, p. 14. Copyright © 2006 off our backs, inc. Reproduced by permission.

As you read, consider the following questions:

1. According to Hoppen, how did the number of accused sex offenders in the army who were given administrative punishments differ from the number court-martialed?

2. How do the experiences of sexually assaulted women in the civilian and the military communities differ, in the author's view?

3. According to a Miles Foundation report, as cited by Hoppen, what percentage of sexual assault offenders are honorably discharged?

When a woman joins the military and attends the basic training of her respective branch ... every element of that training hinges on one primary principle. That principle is camaraderie. One soldier always protects another soldier's back. Everything is about unity and uniformity. The rhythm of cadence is the rhythm of the day. Imagine the devastation, then, of being an American soldier who is assaulted or raped by one of her own, a fellow soldier. Camaraderie becomes cruel captivity.

Investigating Sexual Violence in the Military

Events such as the 1991 Tailhook Association convention, in which more than 100 officers sexually assaulted and harassed dozens of fellow female soldiers but were never convicted; the 1997 sexual assault scandal at the Aberdeen Proving Ground in Maryland; and the 2003 sexual assault scandal at the Air Force Academy have brought the issue of military sexual assault and abuse to the forefront. However, in the past the issue has faded from attention quickly, with the military pledging to police its own, plan for prevention, and clean up the mess.

Little seems to have changed though. An official Department of Defense report states that, "Thirty percent of female veterans in a recent survey reported rape or attempted rape during active duty. Thirty-seven percent of women who reported a rape or attempted rape had been raped more than once; fourteen percent of the victims reported having been gang raped." This is a disturbing reality during a time when 15 percent of our nation's armed forces are female, with more than 204,500 American women serving in the military. The November 23, 2003, article in the *Denver Post*, "Protect Women in Military," reports that, "Nearly one-third of the women in the military have reported a rape or attempted rape, compared with 18 percent in the civilian world. [From 1996 to 2006], twice as many accused sex offenders in the Army were given administrative punishments as were court-martialed." Female soldiers are betrayed by the chain-of-command that is their only line to justice.

Only after the *Denver Post* launched a nine-month investigation into rape and sexual assault against female soldiers in the U.S. military, and then published a three-day series, entitled "Betrayal in the Ranks," from November 16 though November 18, 2003, did Congress and the general public wake up to the terrors that many of our female soldiers face from their fellow soldiers. What the *Denver Post* revealed is an obvious military cover-up that has spanned decades, with reporters discovering that ". . . military commanders routinely fail to prosecute those accused of sexual assault and domestic violence. Nearly 5,000 alleged sex offenders, including alleged rapists, avoided prosecution in the Army the past decade when commanders handled their cases administratively instead of through their criminal courts."

A Unique Form of Sexual Trauma

Military sexual trauma (MST) occurs not only during wartime, but during peacetime as well. Compared with women in the civilian community who face the same experiences, the experiences of women In the military are most definitely unique. The military itself is a microcosm of patriarchal society, isolated from most of civilian society and community, including

A Different Standard for Reporting Rape in the Military

Outside the military, a woman can report a crime to police without fear that colleagues at work will find out. Independent prosecutors determine whether a suspect will stand trial. In the armed forces, commanders make those decisions by weighing evidence involving personnel under their supervision, including, at times, the rape victim. That makes women wary of filing complaints.

USA Today, *March 27, 2005.*

its justice system. For women in the military, sexual trauma usually occurs in the very setting in which the victim works and lives—a setting to which the victim must return. Depending on the circumstances, the woman might actually find herself still working with and taking orders from the man who raped her. Imagine the sense of helplessness and powerlessness, as well as the risk for more victimization. If the perpetrator is in the female soldier's chain-of-command, she might even be dependent on him for basic necessities, such as medical or psychological care. The perpetrator might also have control over her career, deciding about evaluations and promotions. Many female soldiers who become victims of MST find themselves in a situation where they must either see the perpetrator every day or sacrifice their career to protect themselves from further trauma.

The cohesion and stigma of camaraderie within the military makes it particularly difficult for women in the military to divulge negative information regarding a fellow soldier. Powerful risk factors for women in the military include young women who enter male-dominated work groups at lower levels of authority, sexual harassment by officers, and unwanted advances while on duty and in sleeping quarters. Many victims are often reluctant to report sexual trauma, or cannot find methods for reporting the experience to those with authority. When military women do report sexual trauma, they are often encouraged to keep silent, further harassed, or not believed. Reports are often ignored, or the female soldier herself is blamed. The daily situation becomes one of invalidation and constant fear. The betrayal is a devastating one for these women, soldiers committed to protect a country that most often doesn't return the favor.

Caring for Sexual Assault Victims

Due to the military's mishandling of sexual assault and trauma, the Veterans Administration [VA] has had to deal with the effects, providing counseling and healthcare to victims of MST. On February 25, 2004, in her testimony before the Senate Armed Services Subcommittee on Personnel, Dr. Susan Mather, Chief Public Health and Environmental Hazards Officer of the Department of Veterans Affairs, stated that, "The Veterans Health Administration has been aware of the issue for women since at least 1991 when there were reports of sexual abuse among women who served in the Gulf War. Jessica Wolfe, who was then working at VA's Center for Post-Traumatic Stress Disorder, reported that 8 percent of the female Gulf War veterans that she surveyed reported attempted or completed sexual assault during their deployment." A sexual victimization study conducted by the Department of Defense in 1995 among the active duty population found that, "Rates of military sexual trauma among veteran users of VA healthcare appear to be even higher than in general military populations. In one study, 23% of female users of VA healthcare reported experiencing at least one sexual assault while in the military." In a personal interview with Sharon Morrison, Clinical Counselor for the Post-Traumatic Stress Disorder Clinic in

Manhattan, she stated, "I have worked with victims of MST from World War II, Vietnam, and Persian Gulf eras, as well as peace-time, and the helplessness that a victim feels when attempting to receive aid and justice within the military realm after an assault or rape becomes just one more trauma."

The Miles Foundation, a private, non-profit organization, provides services to victims of violence associated with the military, tracking and bringing public attention to the problem of sexual harassment and assault in the military. Using statistics gathered from various government reports, the Miles Foundation reports that "75% to 84% of alleged offenders are honorably discharged." Public groups like the Miles Foundation are now pressuring the military to both protect female solders and to provide adequate care for those who fall prey to sexual abuse or harassment. This pressure has forced the Department of Defense to begin to address the issue, such as announcing a new confidentiality policy for sexual assault victims.

The new policy sets guidelines for restricted reporting that "... allows a sexual assault victim, on a confidential basis, to disclose the details of his/her assault to specifically identified individuals and receive medical treatment and counseling, without triggering the official investigative process." [Journalist] Daniel Pulliam reported that in early January 2005, Pentagon officials "delivered a new set of policies designed to improve the system of preventing and responding to sexual assaults in the armed services. Formed in the last three months as a response to legislation enacted after numerous reports of sexual misconduct involving military personnel, the policies include a military-wide definition of sexual assault, the creation of the position of sexual assault response coordinator and victim advocate, and a checklist for uniformed commanders."

Despite these new policies, the question in regard to whether or not the military is even able to rehabilitate itself still remains. This question becomes a disturbing one during a war time in which combat battle lines are less defined, with many female soldiers in combat support units finding themselves vastly outnumbered by male soldiers, facing enemies on both sides. Until public pressure can force the military to both police and punish its own in sexual assault and abuse cases, anyone who has a sister, mother, wife, daughter, niece, aunt serving in the military must worry, and wonder, who's got her back?

"Every day, pedophiles . . . look for ways to contact our children over the Internet."

Internet Sexual Predators Are a Serious Problem

Alberto R. Gonzales

Pedophiles use the Internet not only to contact and sexually assault children but also to sell images of these assaults to others, claims (now former) U.S. attorney general Alberto R. Gonzales in the following viewpoint. These images are also used by pedophiles to groom new victims, he maintains, and because they are permanent records on the Internet, they may haunt victims long after the abuse. Strict penalties for Internet sexual predators and coordinated strategies that involve both law enforcement and Internet service providers will help protect children from sexual abuse on the Internet, Gonzales asserts.

As you read, consider the following questions:

1. According to Gonzales, what has made it easier for offenders to profit from and distribute Internet images of child sexual abuse?

Alberto R. Gonzales, "Prepared of Statement of Attorney General Alberto R. Gonzales Before the Senate Committee on Banking, Housing, and Urban Affairs Concerning Sexual Exploitation of Children on the Internet," September 19, 2006. www.usdoj.gov/archive/ag/testimony.html.

2. What did an August 2006 University of New Hampshire survey Reveal, according to the author?

3. What have state and local investigators and prosecutors told policy makers is a problem with Internet service providers, according to the author?

Every day, pedophiles troll the Internet to see and sell images of child abuse. They also look for ways to contact our children over the Internet. They are hoping to make contact with the very young, the very innocent, to commit unthinkable acts and potentially sell images of those crimes to other pedophiles.

It is unfortunate that one of the greatest inventions of our generation—the Internet—is providing a building ground for these heinous crimes. That is why parents, volunteers and law enforcement must make the Internet a battleground. We must fight every day because predators seek to hurt our kids every day.

As the father of two young boys, this issue is one that I take extremely seriously on both personal and professional levels. . . . We are all aware that a society's ability to protect its children is a critical marker of that society. That is why protecting our children from sexual exploitation on the Internet is a high priority of the Department of Justice.

Confronting the Facts

I know that the issue of child molestation, rape and pornography can be difficult for people to focus on because it is, simply, so terrible. But we cannot turn away to preserve our comfort level. We must confront the brutal facts. For example:

- Virtually all images of child pornography depict the actual sexual abuse of real children. In other words, each image literally documents a crime scene.

- These are not just "pornographic" pictures or videos. They are images of graphic sexual and physical abuse—rape, sodomy and forced oral sex—of innocent children, sometimes even babies.

- The Internet has created a shocking field of competition to see who can produce the most unthinkable photos or videos of rape and molestation. In the perverse eyes of pedophiles and predators, this means the younger, the better.

The Challenge of Policing Cyberspace

Working with federal investigators and advocacy groups, I have seen just how horrific these images can be. I have seen a young toddler tied up with towels, desperately crying in pain, while she is being brutally raped and sodomized by an adult man. I have seen videos of very young daughters forced to have intercourse and oral sex with their fathers and pictures of older men forcing naked young girls to have anal sex. These are shocking images that cry out for the strongest law enforcement response possible. Moreover, these disturbing images are only the beginning of a cycle of abuse. Once created, they become permanent records of the abuse they depict, and can haunt the victims literally forever once they are posted on the Internet. Unfortunately, advances in technology have also made it easier and easier for offenders both to profit from these images and to distribute them to each other. Once images are posted on the Internet, it becomes very difficult to remove them from circulation. Even more disturbing is the fact offenders rely on these images to develop a plan of action for targeting their next victims, and then use the images to groom victims into submission.

The challenge we face in cyberspace was illustrated by a national survey, released in August 2006, conducted by University of New Hampshire researchers for the National Center for Missing & Exploited Children. The study revealed that a

full third of all kids aged 10 to 17 who used the Internet were exposed to unwanted sexual material. Much of it was extremely graphic.

As I mentioned, this battle against child exploitation is a top priority. [In 2006] we launched a program called "Project Safe Childhood" that is helping to coordinate the good efforts of U.S. Attorneys offices, law enforcement and advocacy groups. Through Project Safe Childhood we are constantly expanding our efforts to address the sexual exploitation of children on the Internet and the financial underpinnings of this exploitation. The program is helping law enforcement and community leaders develop a coordinated strategy to prevent, investigate, and prosecute sexual predators, abusers, and pornographers who target our children.

As we've looked at ways to improve the law enforcement response to the problem of online exploitation and abuse of children, one thing we've continuously heard from state and local investigators and prosecutors is that many Internet Service Providers don't retain records for a sufficient period of time. [In the summer of 2006], I asked a working group within the Department [of Justice] to look at this issue, and we're working hard on ways to remedy this problem.

A Three-Legged Stool

I see the initiative to protect our children as a strong, three-legged stool: one leg is the federal contribution led by United States Attorneys around the country; another is state and local law enforcement, including the outstanding work of the Internet Crimes Against Children task forces funded by the Department's Office of Justice Programs; and the third is non-governmental organizations, like the Financial Coalition Against Child Pornography and the National Center for Missing and Exploited Children—without which we would not have the Cybertipline. . . .

Congress has also provided invaluable support for our efforts by passing the Adam Walsh Child Protection and Safety Act of 2006. The Adam Walsh Act, signed by the President [George W. Bush in] July [2006] helps us keep our children safe by preventing these crimes and by enhancing penalties for these crimes across the board.

None of our efforts can stand alone. All must involve high levels of sharing and coordination. That is what Project Safe Childhood is all about.

One final note that I'd like to share . . . is that our fight against the proliferation of child sexual exploitation on the Internet does not stop at our borders. It demands a global strategy. This makes it imperative that we pay attention to the laws governing child sexual exploitation in other nations. Many countries have astonishingly lenient punishments for child pornography offenses. For instance, in several nations the production of child pornography is punished with only a fine or imprisonment of less than six months or a year. Simple possession is punishable merely by a fine. Just as we need some states to strengthen their laws to punish child sex offenders, we must encourage some foreign lawmakers to strengthen their laws as well, including those concerning the financial components of these crimes.

> *"Most sexually abused children are not victims of convicted sex offenders nor Internet pornographers."*

The Problem of Internet Sexual Predators Is Exaggerated

Benjamin Radford

Most children are not abused by strangers on the Internet but by someone they know, argues Benjamin Radford in the following viewpoint. Despite any hard evidence, he claims, the news media nevertheless create the misleading impression that Internet predators pose a serious threat to America's children. In fact, Radford asserts, the real threat to America's children is parental abuse and neglect. The myth of the ubiquitous Internet sexual predator deflects attention from this real problem, he reasons. Radford, managing editor of Skeptical Inquirer *magazine, is author of* Media Mythmakers: How Journalists, Activists, and Advertisers Mislead Us.

As you read, consider the following questions:

1. In Radford's opinion, what has spawned an unprecedented slate of new sex offender laws?

Benjamin Radford, "Predator Panic: Reality Check on Sex Offenders," *LiveScience*, May 16, 2006. www.livescience.com. Reproduced by permission.

2. How many of the unwanted sexual solicitations reported by teens in the 2001 Youth Internet Safety Survey led to actual sexual contact or assault, according to the author?

3. In the author's view, why are efforts to separate sex offenders from the public of little value?

If you believe the near-daily news stories, sexual predators lurk everywhere: in parks, at schools, in the malls—even in teens' computers. A few rare (but high-profile) incidents have spawned an unprecedented slate of new laws enacted in response to the public's fear.

Responding to Public Fear

Every state has notification laws to alert communities about released sex offenders. Many states have banned sex offenders from living in certain areas, and are tracking them using satellite technology. Officials in Florida and Texas plan to bar convicted sex offenders from public shelters during hurricanes.

Most people believe that sex offenders pose a serious and growing threat. According to [now former] Senate Majority Leader Bill Frist, "the danger to teens is high." On the April 18, 2005, "CBS Evening News" broadcast, correspondent Jim Acosta reported that "when a child is missing, chances are good it was a convicted sex offender." (Acosta is incorrect: If a child goes missing, a convicted sex offender is actually among the *least* likely explanations, far behind runaways, family abductions, and the child being lost or injured.)

On his "To Catch a Predator" series on "Dateline NBC," reporter Chris Hansen claims that "the scope of the problem is immense" and "seems to be getting worse." In fact, Hansen stated, Web predators are "a national epidemic."

Anecdotal Data

The news media emphasizes the dangers of Internet predators, convicted sex offenders, pedophiles, and child abductions. Despite relatively few instances of child predation and little hard data on topics such as Internet predators, journalists invariably suggest that the problem is extensive, and fail to put their stories in context. The "Today Show," for example, ran a series of misleading and poorly designed hidden camera "tests" to see if strangers would help a child being abducted.

New York Times reporter Kurt Eichenwald wrote a front-page article about Justin Berry, a California teen who earned money as an underage Webcam model, seduced by an online audience who paid to watch him undress. Berry's story made national news, and he appeared on Oprah and in front of a Senate committee. Berry's experience, while alarming, is essentially an anecdote. Is Berry's case unique, or does it represent just the tip of the sexual predation iceberg? Eichenwald is vague about how many other teen porn purveyors like Berry he found during his six-month investigation. Three or four? Dozens? Hundreds or thousands? Eichenwald's article states merely that "the scale of Webcam pornography is unknown," while suggesting that Berry's experience was only one of many. (Acosta, Hansen, and Eichenwald did not respond to repeated requests for clarification of their reporting.)

Sex offenders are clearly a threat and commit horrific crimes, but how great is the danger? After all, there are many dangers in the world—from lightning to Mad Cow Disease to school shootings—that are real but very rare. Are they as common—and as likely to attack the innocent—as most people believe? A close look at two widely-repeated claims about the threat posed by sex offenders reveals some surprising truths.

Misleading Statistics

According to a May 3, 2006, "ABC News" report, "One in five children is now approached by online predators."

This alarming statistic is commonly cited in news stories about the prevalence of Internet predators. The claim can be traced back to a 2001 Department of Justice study issued by

Few Sex Offenders Rearrested for Sex Crimes

Less than 4 percent of the sex offenders released from prison in the U.S. in 1994 were reconvicted of a new sex crime within three years of their release. Sexual assault is considered an underreported crime, however, and actual recidivism rates may be higher than indicated below. Studies of released sex offenders over longer periods of time show greater recidivism rates.

	Percentage of Released Sex Offenders		
Recidivism Measure	Child Molesters	Rapists	Statutory Rapists
Within 3 years following release:			
Rearrested for any new sex crime	5.1%	5.0%	5.0%
Reconvicted for any new sex crime	3.5%	3.2%	3.6%
Total realeased	4,295	3,115	443

TAKEN FROM: "Recidivism of Sex Offenders Released From Prison in 1994," Bureau of Justice Statistics, November 2003.

the National Center for Missing and Exploited Children ("The Youth Internet Safety Survey") that asked 1,501 American teens between 10 and 17 about their online experiences. Among the study's conclusions: "Almost one in five (19 percent) . . . received an unwanted sexual solicitation in the past year." (A "sexual solicitation" is defined as a "request to engage in sexual activities or sexual talk or give personal sexual information that were unwanted or, whether wanted or not, made by an adult." Using this definition, one teen asking an-other teen if she is a virgin—or got lucky with a recent date—could be considered "sexual solicitation.")

Not a single one of the reported solicitations led to any actual sexual contact or assault. Furthermore, almost half of the "sexual solicitations" came not from "predators" or adults but from other teens. When the study examined the type of Internet "solicitation" parents are most concerned about (e.g., someone who asked to meet the teen somewhere, called the teen on the telephone, or sent gifts), the number drops from "one in five" to 3 percent.

This is a far cry from a "national epidemic" of children being "approached by online predators." As the study noted, "The problem highlighted in this survey is not just adult males trolling for sex. Much of the offending behavior comes from other youth [and] from females." Furthermore, most kids just ignored (and were not upset by) the solicitation: "Most youth are not bothered much by what they encounter on the Internet. . . . Most young people seem to know what to do to deflect these sexual 'come ons.'" The reality is far less grave than the ubiquitous "one in five" statistic suggests.

Recidivism Revisited

Much of the concern over sex offenders stems from the perception that if they have committed one sex offense, they are almost certain to commit more. This is the reason given for why sex offenders (instead of, say, murderers or armed robbers) should be monitored and separated from the public once released from prison.

The high recidivism rate among sex offenders is repeated so often that it is usually accepted as truth, but in fact recent studies show that the recidivism rates for sex offenses is not unusually high. According to a U.S. Bureau of Justice Statistics study ("Recidivism of Sex Offenders Released from Prison in 1994"), just five percent of sex offenders followed for three years after their release from prison in 1994 were arrested for another sex crime. A study released in 2003 by the Bureau found that within three years, 3.3 percent of the released child molesters were arrested again for committing another sex crime against a child. Three to five percent is hardly a high repeat offender rate.

In the largest and most comprehensive study ever done of prison recidivism, the Justice Department found that sex offenders were in fact *less* likely to reoffend than other criminals. The 2003 study of nearly 10,000 men convicted of rape, sexual assault, and child molestation found that sex offenders had a re-arrest rate 25 percent lower than for all other criminals. Part of the reason is that serial sex offenders—those who pose the greatest threat—rarely get released from prison, and the ones who do are unlikely to re-offend.

If sex offenders are no more likely to re-offend than murderers or armed robbers, there seems little justification for the public's fear, or for the monitoring laws tracking them. (Studies also suggest that sex offenders living near schools or playgrounds are no more likely to commit a sex crime than those living elsewhere.)

Putting the Threat in Perspective

The issue is not whether children need to be protected; of course they do. The issues are whether the danger to them is great, and whether the measures proposed will ensure their safety. While some efforts—such as longer sentences for repeat offenders—are well-reasoned and likely to be effective, those focused on separating sex offenders from the public are of little value because they are based on a faulty premise. Simply knowing where a released sex offender lives—or is at any given moment—does not ensure that he or she won't be near potential victims.

While the abduction, rape, and killing of children by strangers is very, very rare, such incidents receive a lot of media coverage, leading the public to overestimate how common these cases are. Most sexually abused children are not victims of convicted sex offenders nor Internet pornographers, and most sex offenders do not re-offend once released. This information is rarely mentioned by journalists more interested in sounding alarms than objective analysis.

One tragic result of these myths is that the panic over sex offenders distracts the public from a far greater threat to children: parental abuse and neglect.

The vast majority of crimes against children are committed not by released sex offenders, but instead by the victim's own family, church clergy, and family friends. According to the National Center for Missing and Exploited Children, "based on what we know about those who harm children, the danger to children is greater from someone they or their family knows than from a stranger." If lawmakers and the public are serious about wanting to protect children, they should not be misled by "stranger danger" myths and instead focus on the much larger threat inside the home.

| "'*Crying rape*' *[makes]* *every woman who is a victim less credible and less likely to receive justice from the police or the public.*"

False Reports of Sexual Violence Hurt the Real Victims

Wendy McElroy

When women make false rape allegations, they threaten the credibility of real rape victims, claims Wendy McElroy in the following viewpoint. Moreover, she asserts, such claims frighten women in the community and waste local law enforcement resources. If feminists insist that all women's allegations of rape be believed, McElroy reasons, they encourage false accusations. Indeed, if false claims lead to women being viewed as liars, true victims will not be believed, she maintains. McElroy, an editor and columnist, is author of Sexual Correctness: The Gender-Feminist Attack on Women.

Wendy McElroy, "False Rape Claim Hurts Real Victims," *LewRockwell.com*, April 21, 2005. Copyright © 2005 Wendy McElroy. Reproduced by permission of the publisher and author.

As you read, consider the following questions:

1. According to McElroy, how did the Winter Park Police Department and the Rollins College dean respond to Desiree Nall's allegation of rape?

2. Why do NOW-style feminists insist that women do not lie about rape, according to the author?

3. In the author's opinion, what should taking a rape accusation seriously mean?

On April 8, [2005,] the president of the Brevard, Fla., chapter of the National Organization for Women [NOW] was charged by the Florida state attorney's office with filing a false rape report and making a false official statement.

She could be imprisoned for one year on each count and forced to pay for the police investigation she incurred. The case has far-reaching implications for gender politics and for women who report sexual assault in the future.

Examining the Facts

The facts are as follows. On Nov. 17, 2004, part-time Rollins College student Desiree Nall reported being raped in a campus bathroom by two men. The Winter Park Police Department put Rollins on "high alert," advising students to remain indoors when possible.

The dean immediately dispatched a campus-wide email to assure students that extra security measures were being taken.

In a [Rollins College] *Sandspur* article entitled "A Rape Hoax Is No Way to Get Attention," Jean Bernard Chery relates how the incident impacted campus life.

"It was a nightmare for every female student and faculty/staff at Rollins. They were afraid to go to the bathroom or walk on campus alone after dusk.... The incident prompted a candlelight vigil on campus in support of the alleged victim [then unnamed]," Chery wrote.

The Problem of False Allegations

That false allegations are a major problem has been confirmed by several prominent prosecutors, including Linda Fairstein, former head of the New York County District Attorney's Sex Crimes Unit. Fairstein, the author of *Sexual Violence: Our War Against Rape*, says "there are about 4,000 reports of rape each year in Manhattan. Of these, about half simply did not happen."

Craig Silverman, a former Colorado prosecutor known for his zealous prosecution of rapists during his 16-year career, says that false rape accusations occur with "scary frequency." As a regular commentator on the Kobe Bryant trial for Denver's ABC affiliate, Silverman noted that "any honest veteran sex assault investigator will tell you that rape is one of the most falsely reported crimes." According to Silverman, a Denver sex-assault unit commander estimates that nearly half of all reported rape claims are false.

Marc Angelucci and Glenn Sacks,
American Daily, September 17, 2004.

The Price of an Investigation

The police had reason for skepticism. Nall could not assist with composite sketches, offered inconsistent details and did not wish to press charges. An examination at a sexual assault treatment center after the alleged attack produced no evidence of foreign DNA.

Due to publicity and campus panic, however, a police investigation continued at a final estimated cost of more than $50,000. The report of rape was judged a hoax.

According to police, on Nov. 19, Nall phoned and asked to have the case dropped. When Detective Jon Askins questioned her original report, Nall reportedly confessed that she was "not a victim of a sexual batter[y]." The police speculate that Nall, a vocal feminist, may have been trying to "make a statement" about violence against women. The alleged rape occurred during Sexual Assault Awareness Week, which was intended to highlight the issue of sexual violence against women.

Jeff Nall, Desiree's, husband, has been speaking publicly on her behalf. He claims the charges will be appealed on the grounds that an attempted assault did occur. He denies that she confessed to lying. He claims she has been targeted by police because "she is a women's-rights activist."

He also distances NOW from the unfolding fiasco by pointing out that his wife became a chapter president only recently, after the incident. Moreover, according to one article in the *Sandspur*, he argues "that sexual assault cases such as this are not one of the platforms of NOW."

Gender Politics

NOW apparently wishes to maintain distance as well. As of [April 19, 2005], searching its website for the term "Nall" returns no results. After all, NOW has argued that women do not lie about rape. Catharine MacKinnon—a founding mother of the gender feminism that NOW promotes—stated in her book, *Feminism Unmodified*, "The reason feminism uncovered this reality [of male oppression], its methodological secret, is that feminism is built on believing women's accounts of sexual use and abuse by men."

If this methodology is debunked, if women are viewed as no more or less likely to lie than men, then the foundation of gender politics collapses.

It is premature and grandiose, however, to see the collapse of gender feminism within the Nall news story. A false account of rape in a bathroom is a much smaller and more tawdry tale: a tempest in a toilet.

An Unintended Result

Assuming that Nall lied, she has achieved the opposite of what I believe she intended. By "crying rape" she has made every woman who is a victim less credible and less likely to receive justice from the police or the public. She has made women less safe.

Rollins student Elizabeth Humphrey states the point simply: "Lying about that story is absolutely horrible because women are victimized every day. And if we get the reputation of lying, then people won't start to believe us if it does happen."

Instead of publicizing sexual violence against women, Nall has spotlighted the problem of false accusations against men. Her case also raises the question of whether NOW-style feminists encourage false accusations when they flatly insist that women must be believed.

In the '60s, feminists fought to have rape taken seriously. But taking an accusation seriously is not the same as granting it automatic validity. Rather, it means investigating the facts and weighing them in an unbiased manner that favors no one and nothing but the truth. . . .

The definition and legal status of rape within our society continues to evolve. Where it comes to rest depends largely upon the honesty—not the NOW-like silence—with which women confront the problem of false accusations.

| "Of the [sexual] assaults reported the overwhelming majority are legitimate reports."

False Reports of Sexual Violence Are Not Common

Cathleen Wilson

The number of false rape reports is small and no greater than false reports of any other crime, asserts Cathleen Wilson in the following viewpoint. In fact, she maintains, the number reported may be even smaller, as rape is the most underreported violent crime. Rare, high-profile false rape allegations regretfully erect another barrier that keep real victims from coming forward, Wilson argues. Following through on a claim of rape is a difficult journey that most women would not travel simply to seek revenge or attention, she claims. Wilson is executive director of the Women's Rape Crisis Center in Burlington, Vermont.

As you read, consider the following questions:

1. In Wilson's view, what is the one question that will not make headlines?

2. According to the author, what do victims face when seeking justice in our legal system?

Cathleen Wilson, "Free False Reports of Sexual Violence," *Burlington Free Press*, May 18, 2007. Reproduced by permission.

3. In the author's opinion, why do we need to believe rape victims?

In the wake of the Duke [University] lacrosse case,[1] there are many questions that remain unanswered. What actually happened that night? Did the prosecutor have hidden motives? And who, in all of this, is the "victim?"

Yet the one question that will not make headlines is the one that has, perhaps, the biggest implications for all of us. Do high-profile cases such as these discourage other victims from coming forward? Do we take a step backwards in our fight to end sexual violence when such a public rape case turns into a media circus?

The Impact of High-Profile Cases

Sexual violence in our community plays out every day in the lives of our neighbors. [In 2006], the Women's Rape Crisis Center [in Burlington, Vermont] served 602 survivors and their loved ones, marking a 40 percent increase over the [preceding] two years! Although these numbers seem overwhelming for our small community, this number represents a small portion of survivors in our community as sexual assault is the most under-reported of violent crimes. It is estimated that on average only 20 to 30 percent of sexual assaults are reported to law enforcement.

There are a multitude of barriers that prevent many victims from coming forward. Sometimes it is shame, fear of retribution, or past experiences "in the system" that prevent victims from reporting. Yet, I have to wonder, do examples like the Kobe Bryant case[2] and the Duke case serve as further bar-

1. The March 2006 rape charges against three Duke University lacrosse players were dropped on April 11, 2007. The players were declared innocent, the victims of an unethical prosecutor who has since been disbarred for "dishonesty, fraud, deceit and misrepresentation."

2. The criminal rape case was dropped on September 1, 2004. The civil case against Bryant was settled on March 1, 2005.

An Underreported Crime

Despite a steep increase in rape research and public education in the past 30 years, rape continues to be largely underreported. Only one in five women who were raped as adults reported their rape to the police. Fear of their rapist, embarrassment, and not considering their rape a crime or police matter were the primary reasons women chose not to report their victimization to the police.

These findings underscore the need for law enforcement agencies and victim service providers to expand their services to rape victims and do more to convince them that reporting their rape to the police is worthwhile and appropriate.

Patricia Tjaden and Nancy Thoennes,
National Institute of Justice, January 2006.

riers to victims who are thinking of coming forward? These cases have painted an inaccurate portrait of victims that is completely inconsistent with our experiences of working with survivors for over 34 years. Survivors are ordinary people who have been put through the most extraordinary of circumstances.

A Challenging Legal Process

Our legal system is set up in such a way as to put the victim on trial—past sexual experiences, mental health history etc.— all can be thrown into the face of a victim seeking justice in the system. For the most vulnerable and disenfranchised victims (those with disabilities, substance abuse issues, mental health histories, etc.) finding justice as a sexual assault survivor is twice as daunting. They do not fit the profile of a "good" and "innocent" victim. Many times, in sexual assault cases the victim is assumed guilty until proven innocent.

In addition to this, of the assaults reported the overwhelming majority are legitimate reports. According to the FBI, a very small percentage of reports (1 to 2 percent nationally) are actually "false reports." This is comparable to false report rates of other crimes. Women do not "cry rape" after a regretful sexual experience. Going through the system as a survivor of sexual violence is not an easy process. And although our community makes great efforts to ensure that the process is as painless as possible for survivors, it is still a long and difficult journey through the legal system and one that most would not venture into for the sake of revenge or attention seeking.

Sexual violence continues 365 days a year in our community. Some of the men who have turned into murderers in our community are men who have long histories of violence against women. For their countless victims, there were barriers in coming forward. Perhaps someone did not believe them and so they chose not to report. Let's not wait until rape and murder make our front page again. We need to believe victims today.

Periodical Bibliography

The following articles have been selected to supplement the diverse views presented in this chapter.

Louise Arbour — "Violence Against Children," Office of the United Nations High Commissioner for Human Rights in Nepal, October 11, 2006.

Victoria A. Brownworth — "Fighting Rape on Campus," *Curve*, April 2006.

Alan Greenblatt — "Sex Offenders," *CQ Researcher*, September 8, 2006.

Rod Liddle — "Is Rape a Legal Term or Is It Just a Matter of Opinion?" *Spectator*, April 15, 2006.

Wendy McElroy — "False Rape Accusations May Be More Common than Thought," *Foxnews.com*, May 2, 2006. www.foxnews.com.

Julie Rawe — "How Safe Is MySpace?" *Time*, July 3, 2006.

Patricia Tjaden and Nancy Thoennes — "Extent, Nature and Consequences of Rape Victimization: Findings from the National Violence Against Women Survey," National Institute of Justice, January 2006. www.ojp.usdoj.gov/nij/pubs-sum/210346.htm.

Connie de la Vega and Erika Dahlstrom — "The Global Problem of Child Sexual Abuse and Exploitation," Human Rights Advocates, February 26–March 9, 2007. www.humanrightsadvocates.org/images/DahlstromReportFinal.doc.

Vicki Vopni — "Young Women's Experiences with Reporting Sexual Assault to Police," *Canadian Woman Studies*, Winter 2006.

Washington Post — "Rape Is Rape: No Matter When It Begins," November 27, 2006.

Cathy Young — "Assault Behind Bars," *Reason*, May 2007.

OPPOSING
VIEWPOINTS®
SERIES

CHAPTER 2

What Factors Contribute to Sexual Violence?

Chapter Preface

O f all the issues in the sexual violence debate, the greatest
controversy surrounds its causes. Three generally accepted theories of sexual violence are the feminist, the sociocultural, and the evolutionary biology theories. According to
feminist theory, rape is an extension of the political and economic domination of women by men. Rape, argues oft-quoted
feminist Susan Brownmiller, is "nothing more or less than a
conscious process of intimidation by which all men keep all
women in a state of fear." Sociocultural theory maintains that
rape is the result of cultural influences such as traditions of
male dominance, myths that women secretly want to be raped,
and the desensitization that accompanies repeated exposure to
rape in the media.

One of the most controversial rape theories is the evolutionary biology theory. The theory's greatest champions
are biology professor Randy Thornhill and anthropologist
Craig T. Palmer, coauthors of the controversial book *A Natural History of Rape: Biological Bases of Sexual Coercion.* The
authors "challenge the notion that rape only occurs when
males are taught by their cultures to rape." According to
Thornhill and Palmer, rape occurs across cultures and even
among other species. Moreover, they reject the feminist theory
that rape is an act of violence, not sex. "Sexual stimulation is
a proximate cause of raping and is the common denominator
across rapes of all kinds," Thornhill and Palmer maintain.
They contend that rape is a sexually motivated crime rooted
in the process of evolutionary adaptation. According to natural selection, the authors claim, humans have developed different reproductive strategies. Men are adapted to mate as frequently and with as many women as possible. Men rape, these
theorists claim, because it helps spread their genes. The authors do not believe, however, that rape is inevitable. Indeed,

these theorists suggest that "rape can best be prevented by addressing the environmental factors that lead to rape."

Critics contend that the theory that men rape due to a natural biological urge to procreate is based on flawed reasoning. The theory fails, they argue, because natural selection requires that the offspring of a selected behavior survive. Since the child produced by a rapist would have no male parent, the chances of its survival would be greatly reduced. "The rapist generally operates on a hit-and-run basis—which may be all right for stocking sperm banks, but is not quite so effective if the goal is to produce offspring who will survive in a challenging environment," argues writer and activist Barbara Ehrenreich. Moreover, she maintains, the child's chance of success would be further decreased because its mother would likely be damaged by the rape, making her a less than ideal parent. "Most rape victims suffer long-term emotional consequences—like depression and memory loss—that are hardly conducive to successful motherhood," Ehrenreich reasons. Moreover, she claims, Thornhill and Palmer's claim that women can prevent rape by controlling environmental factors such as their appearance will do nothing to prevent rape. According to Ehrenreich, there is no "evidence that women in miniskirts are more likely to be raped than women in dirndls." In fact, she argues, the opposite is true. "Women were raped by the thousands in Bosnia," she maintains, "and few if any of them were wearing bikinis or bustiers."

Since what a society believes causes rape has a significant impact on the policies designed to punish and to reduce it, these theoretical debates remain heated. The authors in the following chapter debate equally controversial claims concerning the factors that contribute to sexual violence.

| *"Pornography is ... a significant factor in sexual violence."*

Pornography Is a Significant Factor in Sexual Violence

Daniel Weiss

Not only is pornography addictive and destructive to the beliefs and attitudes of those who consume it, pornography contributes to sexual violence, argues Daniel Weiss in the following viewpoint. In fact, studies show that among serial killers and child molesters, the use of pornography is common, he points out. Unfortunately, lax enforcement of laws banning hardcore pornography has allowed the pornography industry to flourish worldwide, Weiss claims. Weiss is a senior analyst for media and sexuality at Focus on the Family, an organization that promotes family values.

As you read, consider the following questions:

1. According to Dr. Victor Cline, as cited by the author, how does addiction to pornography progress?
2. What did two-thirds of divorce lawyers at a meeting of the American Academy of Matrimonial Lawyers conclude about online porn, according to Weiss?

Daniel Weiss, "Pornography: Harmless Fun or Public Health Hazard?" Focus on the Family, May 19, 2005. www.family.org. Used with permission.

3. In the author's opinion, what has been the result of increased culture-wide sexualization?

As we consider pornography and the law, we must answer a foundational question: Does the state have a compelling interest in protecting people from obscene materials?

Folks . . . may agree that the state does have such an interest, but U.S. District Judge Gary Lancaster came to a different conclusion. Dismissing the Justice Department's case against Extreme Associates, a company producing rape and torture films, Lancaster wrote that "the government can no longer rely on the advancement of a moral code . . . as a legitimate, let alone a compelling state interest."

Aside from ignoring clear Supreme Court precedent Lancaster's ruling recognized no harm posed by obscene materials. However this case is ultimately decided, it underscores a declining lack of recognition in legal and cultural realms of pornography's threats to individuals, families, and society.

The Facts on Pornography

Ultimately, for obscenity law to be consistently and effectively enforced, our culture must understand the facts on pornography.

More than 25 years ago, Dr. Victor Cline identified the progressive nature of pornography addiction. Once addicted, a person's need for pornography escalates both in frequency and in deviancy. The person then grows desensitized to the material, no longer getting a thrill from what was once exciting. Finally, this escalation and desensitization drives many addicts to act out their fantasies on others. . . .

Medical experts corroborated Cline's early breakthroughs. New technology is allowing doctors to look inside addicts' brains to determine just how damaging pornography is. The witnesses described research showing the similarity of porn addiction to cocaine addiction. Further, because images are

Pornography Promotes Myths About Women

There is strong evidence ... to suggest that images convey values and attitudes that have a profound effect on people. The underlying myths that pornography promotes about women include:

- Women are always willing sexual partners, and mean "yes" even when they say "no."

- Children are appropriate sexual partners.

- Women experience sexual pleasure in being raped.

- Women like to take postures of sexual submission or sexual servility.

- Women are sexual objects not equal partners in sexual activity.

Ottawa Rape Crisis Center,
"Sexual Violence Facts." www.orcc.net.

stored in the brain and can be recalled at any moment, these experts believe that a porn addiction may be harder to break than a heroin addiction.

Now, no one is seriously advocating the legalization of cocaine or heroin, but somehow the pornography industry has convinced a large segment of the population that viewing porn is not just harmless fun, but is also a fundamental right.

By not calling pornography what it is—highly addictive and destructive material—we are heading for troubled times. Dr. Patrick Carnes, a leading researcher on sex addiction, estimates that 3 to 6 percent of Americans are sexually addicted. That's as many as 20 million people.

A Cause of Family Breakdown

This epidemic isn't confined to individuals, however. Pornography is one of the leading causes of family breakdown today.

Two-thirds of the divorce lawyers attending a 2002 meeting of the American Academy of Matrimonial Lawyers said excessive interest in online porn contributed to more than half of the divorces they handled that year. They also said pornography had an almost non-existent role in divorce just seven or eight years earlier.

A poll conducted through my own organization's Web site found that 50 percent of more than 50,000 respondents had been negatively affected by pornography.

This devastation isn't confined to adults either. The Justice Department estimates that nine of 10 children between the ages of 8 and 16 have been exposed to pornography online. Software company Symantec found that 47 percent of school-age children receive pornographic spam on a daily basis, and representatives from the pornography industry told Congress' COPA [Child Online Protection Act] Commission that as much as 20 to 30 percent of the traffic to some pornographic Web sites are children.

Ralph DiClemente, a behavioral scientist at Emory University, described the danger of this exposure. He said, "[Children] can't just put [porn] into their worldview, because they don't have one." He went on to explain that pornography becomes a building block in a child's mental and emotional development.

When pornography becomes a filter through which the rest of life is understood, serious damage occurs. A 2001 report found that more than half of all sex offenders in Utah were adolescents—and children as young as 8 years old were committing felony sexual assault.

The porn industry fights laws such as the Child Online Protection Act, which requires pornographers to use age verification systems, because they know this flood of pornographic imagery is creating a new generation of consumers.

A Significant Factor in Sexual Violence

This increased culture-wide sexualization is generating incredible public health risks. One in five adults in the United States has an STD [sexually transmitted disease], and 19 million new STD infections occur annually, almost half of them among youth ages 15 to 24.

Pornography is also a significant factor in sexual violence. The FBI reports that the most common interest among serial killers is hardcore pornography. Another study found that 87 percent of child molesters were regular consumers of hardcore pornography. [In May 2005], the nation mourned 8-year-old Jessica DeLaTorre, who was abducted, raped, and murdered by a porn addict who had viewed child pornography at an Internet café the night before.

Many of you may also recall Ted Bundy, the serial killer from Florida. In an interview with Focus on the Family founder Dr. James Dobson, just hours before he was executed, Bundy described how early exposure to pornography consumed him and led him down his murderous path. He said he was ultimately responsible for his actions, but that the messages in pornography primed him for those actions.

A Lack of Enforcement

As horrifying as this is, we should not be surprised. Although the Supreme Court was clear in *Miller v. California* that hardcore pornography enjoys no First Amendment protection, lax federal and state law enforcement has essentially given obscenity the protection denied to it in the Constitution.

This lack of enforcement has allowed a back-alley enterprise to grow into an unprecedented global trade in human persons. Pornography turns people into commodities. Men and women become sexual objects to be bought, sold, used and discarded. The last time the United States recognized human beings as consumer goods, it took a civil war to end it.

We should not be shocked with skyrocketing STD infections or marital and family breakdown. Nor when men rape women and children or even when children rape one another. These developments are entirely consistent with the explosive growth in pornography.

This is not harmless adult entertainment, as some would like us to believe, but a real, measurable and undeniable threat to individuals, families and society. The crucial question before us is not whether or not the state has a compelling interest in protecting society from the harm of pornography, but rather, given the overwhelming evidence of harm, why it chooses to do so little?

> "While hard-core raunch has prolifer-
> ated, sexual assaults have not. Could it
> be that pornography prevents rape?"

The Openness that Accompanies Pornography Reduces Sexual Violence

Steve Chapman

Sexual violence has declined, maintains Steve Chapman in the following viewpoint. One explanation for this decline, he argues, is a sexual openness and honesty that has accompanied changing attitudes toward pornography. As a result of sexual openness, people are more willing to talk to children about sex and teach them that there is no excuse for rape and that no one should touch them inappropriately, Chapman asserts. This knowledge, he reasons, deters predators and encourages victims to speak up. Chapman is a syndicated columnist and editorial writer for the Chicago Tribune.

As you read, consider the following questions:

1. In Chapman's view, what might explain the fact that commentators and politicians said little about the news of a decline in rape?

2. Why do people tend to discount statistics about rape, according to the author?

3. In the author's opinion, why does the "Freakonomics" explanation of the decline in rape fall short?

Predators on the Internet, priests molesting children, Duke lacrosse players accused of rape—judging from the news or TV crime dramas, sexual assault appears to be an endless national epidemic. So powerful is this impression that when evidence emerges to suggest otherwise, Americans may have trouble believing their eyes. But the truth about the incidence of rape and other sex crimes is no mirage: It has declined drastically and is still dropping.

The *Washington Post* . . . reported that since the 1970s, rape has diminished in frequency by some 85 percent. If a major newspaper revealed that rape had increased by 85 percent in the past generation, commentators and politicians would be decrying the fact, pointing fingers and demanding remedies. But this phenomenal success story vanished without a trace—possibly it sounded too good to be true, and perhaps because some people see little to gain from acknowledging the truth.

There is no doubt, though, about the fundamental facts. We tend to discount statistics about rape because many victims don't go to the police. But the best evidence comes from the Justice Department's annual crime victimization survey—which compiles numbers based on interviews with some 75,000 Americans, rather than from police reports. The survey found that in 1979, the rate of rape was 2.8 per 1,000 people over age 11. In 2004, it was 0.4.

Some experts say that because the survey was redesigned in the early 1990s, the most reliable data come from 1993 and after. Even here, though, the trend is the same, with a drop of 75 percent. That translates into hundreds of thousands of rapes that didn't happen.

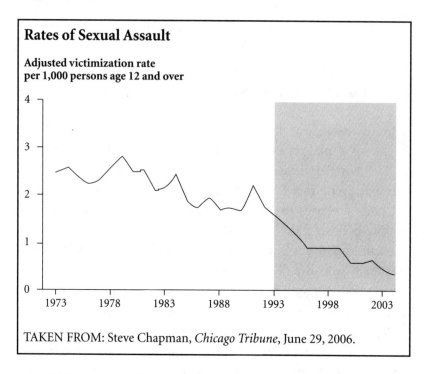

Rates of Sexual Assault

**Adjusted victimization rate
per 1,000 persons age 12 and over**

TAKEN FROM: Steve Chapman, *Chicago Tribune*, June 29, 2006.

The change is part of an overall drop in violent crime, which peaked in 1994. But the progress against sexual assaults has been much larger—and while the FBI says murder, robbery and aggravated assault jumped [in 2005]—rape kept falling. Sexual abuse of children, a plague in the 1980s, has also gotten much less common, with a decline of 47 percent since 1990.

Explaining the Decline

What's going on? [Since the early 1990s], the nation's prison population has doubled, taking many sex offenders out of circulation. The number of people imprisoned for sexually abusing children tripled between 1986 and 1997. According to David Finkelhor and Lisa Jones of the Crimes Against Children Research Center at the University of New Hampshire, "High-frequency offenders are more likely to get incarcerated, so potentially small increases in incarceration of high-volume offenders can have large effects on the overall offense rate."

But imprisonment alone can't explain what's happened. As criminologist Franklin Zimring of the University of California at Berkeley notes, Canada also has seen crime recede—even though its prison population has shrunk. DNA databases have made it easier to catch rapists, but the trend emerged long before they assumed a major role in solving sex crimes.

The "Freakonomics" [a book in which the authors apply economic theory to non-economic issues] explanation—that legal abortion reduced crime by lowering the number of unwanted children, who are more prone to trouble—also falls short. The decline in rape began only seven years after [the landmark abortion rights ruling] *Roe vs. Wade*, and 7-year-olds rarely commit sexual assault. Finkelhor and Jones also note that under the hypothesis proposed by University of Chicago economist Steven Levitt, child abuse should have declined long before the '90s, since parents should be less likely to harm children they wanted.

One theory about the causes of rape, however, has been thoroughly demolished. Among religious conservatives and left-wing feminists, it's an article of faith that pornography leads inexorably to sexual abuse of women and children. But while hardcore raunch has proliferated, sexual assaults have not. Could it be that pornography prevents rape?

In fact, our changing attitudes about erotica are part of a generally more open and honest approach to matters involving sex. And one vital product of that openness has been a willingness to confront questions that were often avoided in the past. Today, kids grow up being taught that "no means no," rapists can't be excused because their victims were dressed provocatively, and adults are never allowed to touch children in certain ways.

Those themes have hardly eradicated this scourge, but they have worked to discourage predators and embolden potential victims. Maybe the main lesson from the decline of sexual assault is an old one: Knowledge is power.

| "*Feminism may be partly to blame [for some sexual violence.]*"

Feminist Messages Contribute to Sexual Violence

Naomi Schaefer Riley

The feminist message that women should be able to engage in the same behavior as men, behavior that sometimes puts them at risk of sexual assault, is partly to blame for sexual violence, claims Naomi Schaefer Riley in the following viewpoint. Feminists who claim that women are never at fault when they are raped, even if they are so intoxicated that they are unable to consent to sex, should discourage behaviors that put them at risk, she reasons. Riley is a Wall Street Journal *editor and author of* God on the Quad.

As you read, consider the following questions:

1. What, in Riley's opinion, were more than a few people thinking in the wake of the rape and murder of Imette St. Guillen?

2. What does the author recommend based on the fact that of the 14 million men in U.S. colleges today, a few will be rapists?

3. Of the college women in the Harvard School of Public Health study who reported being raped, what percentage had been too intoxicated to consent, as cited by Riley?

Word came out [in mid-April 2006] that Darryl Little-john, the New York bouncer charged in the Feb. 25 [2006] rape and murder of graduate student Imette St. Guillen, has been linked by a DNA match to an October [2005] sexual assault on another woman. This latest revelation will no doubt (and rightly) lead to more angry cries about the failure of Mr. Littlejohn's parole officer to keep track of his violent charge and about the negligence of bar owners who do not check the backgrounds of their employees. But it should also serve to remind women, yet again, that it would be a good idea to use a little more common sense.

A police investigation has confirmed that on the night of her murder, Ms. St. Guillen was last seen in a bar, alone and drinking at 3 a.m. on the Lower East Side of Manhattan. It does not diminish Mr. Littlejohn's guilt or the tragedy of Ms. St. Guillen's death to note what more than a few of us have been thinking—that a 24-year-old woman should know better. Yet there are forces in our culture (writing letters to this newspaper even now) that find this suggestion offensive.

The Threats to Women

If you have attended college any time in the past 20 years, you will have heard that if a woman is forced against her will to have sex, it is "not her fault" and that women always have the right to "control their own bodies." Nothing could be truer. But the administrators who utter these sentiments and the feminists who inspire them rarely note which situations are conducive to keeping that control and which threaten it. They rarely discuss what to do to reduce the likelihood of a rape. Short of re-educating men, that is.

But just as sociopaths exist on the Lower East Side, they exist on college campuses. One or two might even be playing lacrosse for Duke University. [April 2006] brought much hand-wringing about the alleged rape of a stripper at a team party in Durham, N.C. Understandably so: An email from one team member, just after the party, suggested that he was aroused by the idea of skinning a woman and killing her. Though the investigation is still under way,[1] commentators have already blamed the event on everything from racism (the stripper was black, the accused players white) to the lack of moral instruction in colleges today.

Which explanation is most credible? Perhaps it doesn't matter. Whatever the problem is, it won't be fixed this year or possibly ever, even with the best sorts of attitude adjustment. Perhaps the law of averages says that, with 14 million men in U.S. colleges today, a few of them will be rapists. What to do? For starters: Be wary of drunken house parties.

Engaging in Dangerous Behavior

Now, readers may well assume that this advice is obvious and that no Duke coed would ever do what the stripper, by her own account, did: Upon finding 40 men at the party instead of the four for whom she agreed to "dance," she stayed and performed anyway. When the partygoers began shouting what she described as racial epithets and violent threats, she left but returned after an apology from a team member. A stripper with street smarts is apparently a Hollywood myth.

But smart women at top schools are engaging in behavior that is equally moronic. In another recent incident, a cadet at the Coast Guard Academy in New London, Conn., apparently got so drunk on two liters of wine and a couple of glasses of beer that she didn't know that she had had sex with a Naval Academy midshipman until he told a friend of hers the next day to get her the morning-after pill.

1. The March 2006 rape charges against the three Duke University lacrosse players were dropped on April 11, 2007. The players were declared innocent, the victims of an unethical prosecutor who has since been disbarred for "dishonesty, fraud, deceit and misrepresentation."

"Rape-Crisis" Feminism

The feminist anti-rape movement emerged in the 1970s for very good reasons. At the time, the belief that women routinely "cry rape" out of vindictiveness or morning-after regrets often caused victims to be treated as if they were the criminals. . . .

"Rape-crisis feminism" . . . replaced one set of prejudices with another. . . .

If feminists want to retain their credibility as advocates for victims of rape, they need to drop the habit of knee-jerk support for every accuser—and to show decency and compassion toward the victims of false accusations.

Cathy Young, Reason, *April 16, 2007.*

In a survey conducted [in 2004] by the Harvard School of Public Health, one in every 20 women reported having been raped in college during the previous seven months. Rape statistics are notoriously unreliable, but the kicker rings true: "Nearly three-quarters of those rapes happened when the victims were so intoxicated they were unable to consent or refuse." And those are just the ones who admitted it.

A Right to Be Taken Advantage Of?

The odd thing is that feminism may be partly to blame. *Time* magazine reporter Barrett Seaman explains that many of the college women he interviewed for his book "Binge" (2005) "saw drinking as a gender equity issue; they have as much right as the next guy to belly up to the bar." Leaving biology aside—most women's bodies can't take as much alcohol as men's—the fact of the matter is that men simply are not, to use the phrase of another generation, "taken advantage of" in the way women are.

Radical feminists used to warn that men are evil and dangerous. [Feminist author] Andrea Dworkin made a career of it. But that message did not seem reconcilable with another core feminist notion—that women should be liberated from social constraints, especially those that require them to behave differently from men. So the first message was dropped and the second took over.

The radical-feminist message was of course wrongheaded—most men are harmless, even those who play lacrosse—but it could be useful as a worst-case scenario for young women today. There is an alternative, but to paraphrase Miss Manners: People who need to be told to use their common sense probably didn't have much to begin with.

"*[Feminist-led programs] note that while minimizing risk is a worthy goal, it is impossible for women to prevent sexual assault.*"

Feminist Messages Aim to Prevent Sexual Violence

Jennifer L. Pozner

Claims that feminists promote rape by encouraging irresponsible behavior are misleading and dangerous, argues Jennifer L. Pozner in the following viewpoint. In fact, she claims, feminist campaigns recommend that women avoid high-risk activities to minimize the risk of rape. The suggestion that women can avoid sexual assaults simply by staying at home and avoiding parties is not an effective rape-prevention strategy, Pozner maintains. In addition, the notion that men are violent and that women should simply accept that fact and live in fear is unacceptable and will not prevent rape. Pozner is founder and executive director of Women in Media and News.

As you read, consider the following questions:

1. According to Pozner, what does Naomi Schaefer Riley conclude in the case of the murder of Imette St. Guillen?

Jennifer L. Pozner, "Columnist Dishes Dangerous Logic About Rape," *Women's eNEWS*, April 26, 2006. www.womensenews.org. Reproduced by permission.

2. What does the author claim was Riley's goal in writing about the St. Guillen rape and murder?

3. In the author's opinion, what is the moral of Riley's story?

Fresh from the media's trusty "feminism is responsible for every evil thing in American culture" files, a new one: feminists cause rape. At least, that's the premise of an April 14 [2006] *Wall Street Journal* opinion piece headlined, "Ladies, You Should Know Better: How feminism wages war on common sense."

Bashing Rape Victims

In the piece, Naomi Schaefer Riley declares women "moronic" for "engaging in behavior" that makes them rape-magnets and feminists responsible for turning women into morons in the first place. She bashes rape and murder victims as too stupid to prevent their attacks and paints an entirely false picture of campus feminist education and advocacy programs.

Learning that DNA evidence links Darryl Littlejohn—the bouncer charged in the high-profile rape and murder of New York graduate student Imette St. Guillen—to a prior sexual assault, Schaefer Riley concludes not that serial rapists must be stopped, but that women should "use a little more common sense" lest they get themselves attacked.

"Ms. St. Guillen was last seen in a bar, alone and drinking at 3 a.m on the Lower East Side of Manhattan," Shaefer Riley writes, and "more than a few of us have been thinking that a 24-year-old woman should know better."

It's hard to imagine that many intelligent adults would look at that brutal rape and homicide and think, "Wow, what a stupid dead girl." But that's the company she keeps. Schaefer Riley's early writing on religion was subsidized by the John M. Olin Foundation, which—before it closed in 2005—gave hundreds of thousands to help female writers such as Christina

Feminists Talk About Risky Behavior

Feminists talk about risky behavior. We were the *FIRST* people to talk about what *WE* call rape avoidance. Every rape crisis center worth its salt, every prevention program I know about talks about the risks of walking alone, walking alone at night, drinking and drugging to excess. It's we feminists who talk about how alcohol use/overuse undermines our ability to resist assault.

Of course we discuss how to avoid stranger rape—we advocate that women and girls learn self-defense, plan ahead, be aware of our surroundings, trust our instincts, partner with other women while jogging.

Susan McGee, editorial, April 2006.
www.ncdsv.org/ncd_newsinterest06.html.

Hoff Sommers, author of "Who Stole Feminism? How Women Have Betrayed Women," produce highly inaccurate polemics and media programs [that] foment the idea that feminists whine too much about rape, that date rape is a "myth" and that the Violence Against Women Act is unnecessary.

Dismisses the Duke Controversy

The author also dismisses the controversy surrounding the 27-year-old African American student and exotic dancer who alleges she was raped by white Duke University lacrosse players as simply "much hand-wringing about the alleged rape of a stripper."

"A stripper with street smarts is apparently a Hollywood myth," Schaefer Riley sniffs, since the woman didn't anticipate the possibility of assault.

With her penchant for victim blaming Schaefer Riley promotes dangerous misperceptions about the nature of rape in America.

While it's certainly important for women (and men) to evaluate our social behavior with an eye toward safety, staying sober and staying home does not inoculate women against sexual violence.

But keeping women safe wasn't Schafer Riley's real goal. Nor were St. Guillen and the alleged Duke U. victim her ultimate targets. She reserved her harshest scorn for feminists, the easy whipping girls of contemporary culture.

Schafer Riley claims feminists have created a culture of female irresponsibility. Feminists, she claims, tell college students that "if a woman is forced against her will to have sex, it is 'not her fault' and that women always have the right to 'control their own bodies.'" Feminists, she says, don't tell women how to avoid particularly threatening situations. Feminists, she says, "rarely discuss what to do to reduce the likelihood of a rape. Short of re-educating men, that is."

The Picture Is Distorted

Problem is, the picture she paints doesn't resemble today's campuses. Contrary to decades of concerted attacks on college feminism, anti-rape education and organizing is very rarely limited to what Schaefer Riley describes as radical feminist warnings "that men are evil and dangerous."

In fact, self-defense classes have become very popular on college campuses, and most schools offer awareness-raising programs on the role alcohol plays in a large percentage of sexual assaults.

Despite Schaefer Riley's suggestion that feminists have promoted hard drinking as a gender equality issue, many women's centers and women's studies programs conduct campaigns to help women avoid potentially high-risk situations, advising students to avoid binge drinking, decline drinks poured by others to avoid date-rape drugs, and to attend parties with one or more friends rather than solo.

The most effective ethical programs—certainly those that are feminist-led—note that while minimizing risk is a worthy goal, it is impossible for women to prevent sexual assault, since the majority of rape cases are perpetrated by victims' boyfriends, husbands, relatives, friends or acquaintances, not bouncers who accost strangers in dark alleys or a gang of drunken lacrosse players.

Ignoring Feminist Efforts

Since such efforts poke a hole in Schaefer Riley's premise, she simply ignores them.

"Whatever the problem is, it won't be fixed this year or possibly ever, even with the best sorts of attitude adjustment," Schaefer Riley writes. "Perhaps the law of averages says that, with 14 million men in U.S. colleges today, a few of them will be rapists. What to do? For starters: Be wary of drunken house parties."

The moral of her story: Women who go out to bars in the city ask for rape. Strippers who work bachelor parties ask for rape. College students who get plastered ask for rape. And men who rape? It's not worth holding them accountable for their behavior.

The contention that men are essentially violent and women just have to learn to deal is a useless strategy for sexual assault prevention. In fact, it's downright dangerous, perpetuating the regressive idea that men can commit abusive, criminal acts with impunity and the only thing women can do to cope is to avoid alcohol, parties and miniskirts. It's a depressing view of the world that offers women no hope of societal change, only fear and disempowerment.

The "common sense" that Schaefer Riley says feminists have trained out of women is sorely missing from her commentary, as it is from most attempts to shift responsibility away from perpetrators and onto victims.

> "Images portrayed of black girls and
> women as gyrating, hypersexual, inso-
> lent, irresponsible, and utterly available
> prey . . . could lead to violence."

Some Rap and Hip-Hop Music Promotes Sexual Violence

Michele Goodwin

*When black rap artists portray African American women as irre-
sponsible prey, they put African American women at risk of
sexual violence, claims Michele Goodwin in the following viewpoint. It is dangerous and destructive to closet public discussion
of rape, incest, and abuse in the African American community
out of fear that it will exacerbate racism when these problems
are graphically portrayed by black artists in the media, Goodwin
maintains. Only when African Americans are made accountable
for these images and behaviors can they change, she reasons.
Michele Goodwin is a professor of law at DePaul University in
Chicago.*

As you read, consider the following questions:

1. Why does Goodwin claim that she is a helicopter parent?

Michele Goodwin, "Take the Debate Over Degrading Rap Videos Off Mute," *Christian
Science Monitor*, August 11, 2006. www.csmonitor.com. Reproduced by permission.

2. Where did the student who called Goodwin's daughter a "stupid ho" learn these terms, according to the author?

3. In the author's opinion, why are African Americans deluding themselves if they think no one notices the African American community's self-destruction?

My daughter is 11 years old. Like other girls her age, she enjoys text messaging, going to movies, and she wants braces. She also happens to be a straight A student, winner of her school's science fair, and an accomplished classical dancer at a premier ballet school in Chicago. She is also African-American. Despite her accomplishments and what some might say is a "good start," I am a helicopter parent (I hover constantly).

Because the horrible images portrayed of black girls and women as gyrating, hypersexual, insolent, irresponsible, and utterly available prey may stigmatize her and could lead to violence against her, I worry. Naively, I assumed this could be managed by monitoring the MTV, VH1, and, worst of all, BET [Black Entertainment Television] channels in our home. Yet, I shouldn't have been surprised when my daughter's new classmate from the Philippines, unprovoked, called my daughter a "stupid ho" and "b-ch," terms of endearment used by some black men in videos and rap music. When confronted by the principal, the boy admitted addressing my daughter that way, but argued in his defense that he learned it from black men on TV.

A controversy [in the summer of 2006] involving Troi Torian (aka DJ Star), a popular New York disc jockey, and his spate of on-air sexual and violent threats against a little girl illustrates the perverse state of affairs. To taunt a rival disc jockey, DJ Star asked callers to reveal the whereabouts of Rashawn Casey's 4-year-old daughter. He made highly descriptive, on-air references to possible sexual interactions

with her. He offered a $500 reward for any information about where the little girl attends school.

Dirty Little Secrets

This kind of lewd public commentary demonstrates a certain kind of 21st-century minstrelsy and reveals a complex state of intraracial affairs. Within the African-American community, issues of sexual violence, including rape, incest, and abuse are typically closeted. Black people seem to fear that if whites were to get wind of such problems it might exacerbate racism and perpetuate stereotypes.

For example, Michael Eric Dyson, winner of the 2006 NAACP [National Association for the Advancement of Colored People] Image Award, has publicly criticized Bill Cosby for exposing dirty little secrets such as drug use, parental neglect, and other issues in the black community. Professor Dyson describes Mr. Cosby as being insensitive and pushing a "destructive" agenda. Dyson claims Cosby won't admit that racism exists. Nothing could be further from the truth than the notion that accountability, integrity, and self-growth are "destructive" to black Americans. Neither are these right-wing, Republican, or "white" values.

Moreover, we are only deluding ourselves to think no one notices this terrible self-destruction. After all, BET is quite public, as are videos on MTV and the criminal records of those caught in the matrix of celebrity and "gangsta" life. Ironically, it remains black men who primarily portray black women as hypersexual. From once exporting images of respected if not noble civil rights leaders and activists, the black image now includes desperate sexual depravity. Most important, I wonder why these conversations must happen in the race closet when the videos and behavior are very public, unapologetic, and ubiquitous.

> *"To focus on hip-hop as the instigator of our coarsening culture is a grievous misdiagnosis."*

Blaming Rap and Hip-Hop for Negative Messages Distracts Us from Dealing with the Real Issues

Salim Muwakkil

While some rap and hip-hop music does contain messages of misogyny and violence, focusing on the music as the cause of these societal ills is the wrong approach, says Salim Muwakkil in the following viewpoint. A 2007 incident in which radio host Don Imus used a derogatory term to describe black female basketball players placed hip-hop music in the spotlight as a contributor to attitudes of disrespect toward women. Hip-hop reflects the social conditions that inspire its negative lyrics, and instead of censoring the lyrics outright, we should channel resources toward improving those conditions. Salim Muwakkil is a senior editor of In These Times.

As you read, consider the following question:

1. What caused society's focus to shift to the more sensationalistic aspects of hip-hop?

2. Which black political and social activist has lent his voice to the Don Imus debate?

3. Does the author feel that communities should not advocate for more respectful and responsible actions by hip-hop artists and record companies?

Perhaps it was inevitable that discussions provoked by the words "nappy-headed hos" would come around to rap music and the culture of hip-hop. After all, hip-hop has taken the rap for just about every social ill: misogyny, gun violence, rampant materialism, anti-Semitism, gang warfare, even the decline of the NBA. Yes, to some extent, the insulting remarks of radio shock-jock Don Imus (who called the Rutgers University women's basketball team "nappy-headed hos," for which he's been fired and subsequently sued) were drawn from a rhetorical subculture influenced by certain strands of rap music. But to focus on hip-hop as the instigator of our coarsening culture is a grievous misdiagnosis.

Hip-hop, at its best, reflects, distills, amplifies, deconstructs and re-contextualizes the social realities that are its raw material. The product of this creation then is reincorporated into that reality. Born in the ghettoes of New York City in the disjuncture between the hopes of the civil rights promise and the harsh realities of economic disinvestment, hip-hop's founding spirit expresses an insurgent rejection of business as usual.

Nevertheless, big business saw great profits in its growing popularity. Large record companies absorbed the independent labels and accelerated hip-hop's profit potential. These companies changed the marketing emphasis from creativity to profitability, which shifted the focus to the more sensation-

The Company We Keep

Negative people, not inappropriate music or entertainment, are the real reason why racism, sexism and homophobia persist in our society. . . . If we associate with those people who have sexist or misogynistic beliefs, we will likely internalize those ideas as our own. If we continue to ignore this fact and instead campaign against hip-hop music or violent video games, we are missing the point.

Michael Kreicher, The Dartmouth, *May 2, 2007.*

alistic aspects of the genre rather than its politically charged or artistically challenging expressions.

Thus, sensationalized tales of drug dealing, sex seeking and gun play (by groups like Oscar winner Three 6 Mafia) find more corporate support than political rappers like Dead Prez or adventurous groups like the Perceptionists. This disproportionate emphasis on pathology has distorted hip-hop's public face.

Thus, when Imus' defenders blamed hip-hop for providing their man the vocabulary for his insult, many agreed. Oprah Winfre's entire response to the Imus affair was a two-segment "town hall" meeting on the state of hip-hop.

Even the Rev. Al Sharpton, president of the National Action Network and leader of the campaign demanding Imus be fired, has linked arms with those protesting demeaning lyrics in hip-hop. On May 3, Sharpton led marches on the corporate offices of Sony-BMG, Universal Music Group and Warner Music Group's to protest their promotion of demeaning rap lyrics.

"This is not about censorship—it is about standards," Sharpton told the crowd at the march's conclusion. "There's a standard that says Ice-T can't rap against police. There's a standard that says you can't rap about gays, and you shouldn't. They had standards against Michael Jackson saying things anti-Semitic. Where is the standard against n-----,' 'ho' and 'bitches'?" Sharpton is a long-time critic of what he considers degrading rap lyrics, but the momentum of the Imus controversy obliged him to raise his voice on the issue.

Others also have been forced to take action in the wake of the shock-jock's fall. The Hip-Hop Summit Action Network (HHSAN), led by former Def Jam Records CEO Russell Simmons and former NAACP Executive Director Benjamin Chavis, has announced a new campaign urging radio stations and other media not to air the words "bitch," "ho" and "n-----."

Chavis noted that the HHSAN directive is not for rappers to stop using the words. "We don't want to violate the First Amendment Rights to free speech," Chavis told the National Newspaper Publishers Association. But other crusaders are not that fastidious. They want to force rappers to stop saying things they do not like. Like their fellow citizens, African Americans have to be reminded that the urge to censor is an authoritarian impulse.

One of the most salient aspects of both the Communist Soviets and Nazi Germans was their demand for artistic conformity. Of course, that should not deter the African-American community from agitating for respectful media depictions, for more responsibility from artists, or for holding record companies accountable for violating community standards.

Yet Russell Simmons, who sometimes seems in thrall to corporate interests, was on target when he told Oprah that we have to let rappers reflect what they see. "People who are angry . . . and come from tremendous struggle; they have poetic license, and when they say things that offend you, you have to talk about the conditions that create those kinds of lyrics."

In a black America that is largely fatherless, resource-starved mothers may come across as promiscuous gold-diggers to their proud but clueless sons, who may turn into rappers and tell their tales. We might better channel social resources if we listened more attentively to those tales, Granted, too many performers are "false flagging" their woes for profit, but there's still plenty of wheat amidst the chaff.

Periodical Bibliography

The following articles have been selected to supplement the diverse views presented in this chapter.

Stephen Baskerville	"Leftist Ideologues Have Corrupted U.S. Judicial System," *Human Events*, October 29, 2007.
Johnnetta B. Cole	"What Hip-Hop Has Done to Black Women," *Ebony*, March 2007.
Richard Jerome	"Faces of Rape: Helping Rape Victims Come Out of Hiding and Tell Their Stories," *People Weekly*, March 20, 2006.
Michael Kreicher	"Ain't Nuthin' but a Blame Game," *Dartmouth*, May 2, 2007. http://thedartmouth.com/2007/05/02/opinion/kreicher/.
Mike Males	"The Decline of Rape," *Los Angeles Times*, February 18, 2007.
New York Times	"Turning Back the Clock on Rape," September 23, 2006.
Melinda Tankard Reist	"An Invasion of Pornography," *Online Opinion*, July 23, 2007. www.onlineopinion.com.au/view.asp?article=6114.
Laura Sessions Stepp	"A New Kind of Date Rape," *Cosmopolitan*, September 2007.
Cathy Young	"On Campus, an Absurd Overregulation of Sexual Conduct," *Boston Globe*, May 22, 2006.
Femke van Zeijl	"War Against Women: Many Thousands of Women Have Been Raped in Darfur—Yet They Are the Ones Who End Up Being Punished," *New Internationalist*, June 2007.

OPPOSING
VIEWPOINTS®
SERIES

CHAPTER 3

How Should Society Respond to Sexual Violence?

Chapter Preface

Societies have historically viewed sexual violence as a crime by and against individuals. In fact, most societies have dealt with sexual violence by attempting to control the behavior of individuals. For example, rape prevention programs teach women how to avoid rape, and community programs teach children how to recognize and protect themselves from potential predators. Perpetrator control most often focuses on punishment, a notion that is based on the long-held belief that people will avoid criminal behavior to avoid punishment. Some argue, however, that despite severe punishments for these crimes, sexual violence remains a serious problem. These commentators claim that to reduce rape, one of the most common forms of sexual violence, society must view it as a social, rather than as an individual problem.

Those who believe that rape is a social problem assert that victim and perpetrator controls do not work. "Victim control teaches women to avoid rape, but doesn't reduce the threat of rape," argues the Rape Prevention Education Program (RPEP) at the University of California–Davis. Even if women avoid risky situations and behavior, they cannot always avoid being raped, RPEP asserts. Critics of efforts to control the rapist with the threat of severe punishment claim that such policies confuse prosecution with prevention. "There is little evidence that punishment serves as a deterrent," RPEP maintains. Addressing the social problem—the inequality between men and women—is a more effective way to reduce rape and other forms of sexual violence, these analysts argue. "Rape prevention techniques are very important in decreasing the vulnerability of individuals," RPEP asserts, "but in order to eliminate the occurrence of rape from our society, we must first examine its cause more deeply so that we can take collective action."

Those who see rape as a social problem argue that rape results from the inequality between men and women. Rape, they maintain, is an inevitable result of a male-dominated society. According to psychology and women's studies professor Sandra Lipsitz Bem, rape is simply an exaggeration of everyday male dominance. "The sexual brutalization of a woman by a man," Bem asserts, "is not just an isolated act, a case of an individual man taking out his psychological problems on an individual woman. It is rather the inevitable cultural by-product of an androcentric heterosexuality that eroticizes sexual inequality." Bem cites as evidence that male dominance is considered normal and natural heterosexuality. Neither men nor women prefer "heterosexual relationships in which the woman is bigger, taller, stronger, older, smarter, higher in status, more experienced, more educated, more talented, more confident, or more highly paid than the man," Bem explains.

To reduce rape and eliminate women's vulnerability to rape requires altering the power relationship between women and men, these observers maintain. "The whole assumption of male superiority will have to be negated," RPEP maintains. To reduce inequality between men and women will also require a change in female socialization. Teaching self-defense, promoting equal opportunities, and encouraging women to engage in sports will help to reduce perceptions of inequality. "Women need to learn direct and appropriate responses which reflect a seriousness about their refusal to be intimidated," RPEP reasons.

Whether society should view sexual violence as an individual or a social problem remains in dispute. The authors in the following chapter debate other controversial ways each believes society should respond to sexual violence.

> *"Questioning [the victim's behavior] ...*
> *blames the victim for her actions,*
> *rather than focusing on the actions of*
> *the attacker."*

Society Should Not Blame the Victim for Sexual Violence

Laura Pedro

In the following viewpoint, Laura Pedro asserts that when women walking alone are sexually assaulted and murdered, society offers the same ineffective solution—women should not walk home alone. This attitude blames the victim, when the real solution is to stop the sexual predators, she claims. Moreover, Pedro maintains, walking home with a man is not always safe since more than half of women who are raped are assaulted by someone they know. Asking women to change their behavior does not prevent sexual violence, she reasons; it promotes fear of and dependence on men. Pedro is a staff writer for the Vermont Cynic, *the University of Vermont's student newspaper.*

As you read, consider the following questions:

1. In Pedro's opinion, why do women have a reason to be afraid?

Laura Pedro, "No Easy Answers to Sexual Violence," *Vermont Cynic*, October 30, 2006. www.vermontcynic.com. Reproduced by permission.

2. According to the National Violence Against Women survey, as cited by the author, what percentage of women who survive a rape or attempted rape are assaulted by someone they know?

3. As related by the author, what overshadowed one University of Vermont sophomore's concern for her own well-being after she may have been raped by a male friend?

Gender violence has never been a more prevalent issue than it is today. In the wake of the abduction and murder of Michelle Gardner-Quinn,[1] which was seemingly if not undeniably sexually motivated, and recent headlining of sexual assault cases, women have reason to be afraid.

Now women must become aware.

A Reason to Be Afraid

The gunman who took ten female hostages in an Amish schoolhouse [in October 2006] singled out the girls, aged six to 13, and forced all older women and males to leave the room. Press reports say that the attack was sexually motivated.

Several weeks earlier, a middle aged man took six girls hostage in a Colorado classroom, and in the same manner, hand picked "small girls, many with blond hair." Press reports confirm that the gunman "sexually assaulted and traumatized" some of the victims.

These attacks represent the consistent trend of young girls being targeted for sexual assault. Statistics from the National Violence Against Women survey found that 21.6 percent of women who survived rape were under the age of 12, and 32.4 percent were between the ages 12 to 17.

Now the problem that once loomed in the distance has hit home. Females in Burlington [Vermont] fear walking alone

1. Gardner-Quinn was an undergraduate at the University of Vermont who was kidnapped and murdered in the early hours of October 7, 2006, while walking home to her dorm after a night out with friends.

Asking the Wrong Questions

Society always asks questions like "Why did she talk to strangers?" "Why was she alone?" "Why was she dressed like that?" "Why was she drinking, and why did she leave that drink unattended?". . .

Why don't you ask, "Why did he rape her?" Is that too obvious of a question?

Heather Wilson,
Rocky Mountain Collegian,
September 22, 2005.

downtown, as well as on-campus. Friends of mine have refused to come over on school nights because they're afraid of having to walk home alone.

A Dangerous Solution

Over and over again the same solution is offered. Women are told not to walk by themselves; to find a male escort. Is this just a case of replacing one male with another?

Women are told not to walk home alone because of male predators in society. And yet, by asking a male to walk her home, a female faces the same threat.

The survey found that of the 17.6 percent of women who survived a rape or attempted rape, 64 percent were assaulted by a spouse, cohabiting partner, boyfriend, or date. There is no guarantee that the male friend who offers to walk you home won't become the feared sexual assaulter, especially when alcohol is involved.

When examining Gardner-Quinn's murder, questions are brought up, like, why was she walking home alone that night?

This type of questioning is futile and unproductive. It blames the victim for her actions, rather than focusing on the actions of the attacker.

Prevention for women is important, but it is men's actions that need to change.

Women should not take this step backward, a step towards dependence. The threat of gender violence should be acknowledged by women, but it should not control their lives.

Sending Inconsistent Messages

Tragedies like the ones that have occurred in [October 2006], bring to the surface the larger issue of women trusting men. Women are told to be dependent on men, and at the same time to fear them. The message is not consistent.

A [University of Vermont] sophomore, who we'll call Rachel, experienced an incident of assault many other women can relate to. After drinking at a party downtown, she decided to stay with a male acquaintance who offered her a place to sleep so she didn't have to walk back up to campus.

The next morning she woke up with no shirt on, her pants unbuttoned, and no recollection of what had occurred with the male acquaintance the night before.

Feeling embarrassed and uncomfortable about her actions, she didn't ask him what happened. The victim's concern for her own well-being was overshadowed by shame produced by societal standards. Wanting to forget the experience and not think about it any further, Rachel never questioned what occurred, a decision she now regrets.

There is no easy solution to gender violence. Men and women need to recognize that male violence towards women is an imperative issue, and it needs to stop.

| "*Certain forms of behaviour on the part of women will lead to an increased risk of sexual assault from men.*"

Some Victims Are Partly Responsible for Sexual Violence

Rod Liddle

Certain types of risky behavior, such as heavy drinking and wearing seductive clothing, increase a woman's chances of being raped, claims Rod Liddle in the following viewpoint. While these risky behaviors do not release a rapist from guilt, Liddle asserts, women must assess the risks and take responsibility for their behavior. Liddle is a TV documentarian and editor of the Spectator, *a conservative British magazine of news and commentary.*

As you read, consider the following questions:

1. In Liddle's view, how did activists characterize the one-third of the British public who said women were partially responsible for being raped?

2. To what possible scenario in his own life does the author compare a woman's decision to get drunk, flirt, and dress provocatively?

3. In the author's opinion, from what segment of the British population did the third that held women partially responsible for being raped come?

There was a clever little opinion poll in [British] morning newspapers [in November 2005] courtesy of Amnesty International UK [United Kingdom]. The headline story from the poll was that about a third of British people thought that women were 'partially or totally responsible' for being raped if they didn't say 'No' clearly enough, or were wearing revealing clothing, or were drunk, or had been behaving in a flirtatious manner.

A Strong Reaction

Usually opinion polls are, well, a matter of opinion: respondents tick a box expressing one view or another and the rest of us can agree or agree to differ. Not with this poll, though. In the manner in which it was reported, there was no doubt: that one third of the country who ticked the 'partially or totally responsible' boxes were quite simply, objectively, plain wrong. Worse than that, they were stupid and dangerous and deserved a good kicking from the relevant authorities. Commenting upon its own poll, Amnesty International UK's Kate Allen said this: 'It is shocking that so many people will lay the blame for being raped at the feet of women, and the government must launch a new drive to counteract this sexist blame culture.' Lordy: that's something to look forward to.

Pretty soon after Kate made her observation and inevitable demand, every charitable organisation with a vague interest in this area was out of the blocks. Victim Support, for example, called the poll alarming and appalling and demanded that the thickoes [thick-headed ones] who had ticked the wrong boxes be 'educated'. The poll was reported (as a lead story) on BBC News 24, and it was assumed throughout—it was a given—that the public had got it all wrong. A regiment of angry

A Woman's Responsibility

A random sample of 1,095 [British] adults were given a series of scenarios and asked to indicate whether they believed a woman was totally responsible, partially responsible or not at all responsible for being raped.

ICM Research for Amnesty International, November 2005.
www.icmresearch.co.uk.

women marched into the television studios to shout things. One particularly vexed lady insisted endlessly that women had 'a right not to be raped'.

Making a Common-Sense Point

At no time during these interviews, or in the newspaper coverage the following morning, was it even whispered that perhaps that 30-odd per cent of British people might have a bit of a point. It's one of the things you're not allowed to say. And yet, given the terms of the poll, common sense would suggest that those sexist blame-culture monkeys, that one third of the British public—pretty much equally divided between men and women, by the way—are entirely right.

The precise question asked by the . . . researchers was this: 'I'm going to read out a series of scenarios which a woman may find herself in. In each, please could you indicate whether you believe a woman is totally responsible, partially responsible or not at all responsible for being raped.' And then followed the list of scenarios: being drunk, flirting, etc.

Now, your response may well depend upon what you understand by the word 'responsible' or, indeed, 'partially responsible'. (Only the real hurters, about the usual 5 or 6 per cent of the poll, put down 'totally responsible', by the way—so

Amnesty International's headlines were technically accurate but nonetheless misleading.) Clearly, if you are a woman who is as drunk as a skunk, flirting outrageously with a man while wearing a boob tube and micro skirt, the likelihood of your being raped is going to be greater than if you stayed at home with a cup of Bovril [instant beef bouillon] watching *Songs of Praise* [a British religious TV program] and dressed like Ann Widdecombe [a conservative, family-values politician in Great Britain].

This does not remotely mitigate the guilt of the rapist, however—and that supposedly errant one third of the British public didn't seem to suggest that it should, either. A comparable scenario might be this: if I go for a walk at midnight in Harlesden [a seedy borough of London known as the gun capital of Britain] wearing a flashy suit and holding aloft a BlackBerry, I would be more likely to be mugged than if I skulked down the street in jeans and trainers [athletic shoes] looking destitute. Or, indeed, better still, did not visit the area at all after sundown. But my comparatively risky behaviour does not lessen by one iota the guilt of my mugger, even though you might argue that I am partially responsible for my own downfall.

You might argue with some force that the mere fact that I should be scared to visit Harlesden after sundown while wearing a suit is a form of oppression in itself. And, similarly, that it is every woman's right to get well and truly plastered and behave like a Dandle Dinmont [terrier] in heat without worrying that she might be attacked as a result—and that such a constraint on behaviour is, indeed, oppressive and unjust, I'd wholly agree—and I suspect the British people who ticked the wrong boxes would agree, too. But it does not alter my contention that certain forms of behaviour on the part of women will lead to an increased risk of sexual assault from men, and that it is silly to pretend otherwise.

Assessing Life's Risks

I stress: of course I do not mean that they should be sexually assaulted or that the sexual assault is in some way justified, or the gravity of the offence even slightly lessened—merely that there is a greater likelihood that an assault will take place. When we take responsibility for ourselves we do not assume that we are living in a perfect world; we assess risk, regardless of how unfair or oppressive that risk might be, and behave accordingly.

I'm not sure what to make of that other scenario put up by Amnesty: the woman who does not say no 'clearly enough'. Do they mean that she didn't say no at all? Or sort of mumbled no, remorsefully, afterwards (as so many of us have done). What about those women who say 'Yes!' with great enthusiasm and gusto? They have rights too, you know.

Interestingly, that errant 30-odd per cent of the British public who insist that we live in the real world—rather than in some fabulous sunlit upland where actions do not lead to consequences because we don't want them to—were drawn almost exclusively from that most sensible tranche of the population: the older working class. . . . I don't think that they'll be easily susceptible to a government re-education drive. They've had to put with a lot of re-educating from governments and pressure groups this last 30 or 40 years and it doesn't seem to have changed their point of view one bit. They continue to take the common-sense point of view, and can usually smell humbug a mile off. They smelled it in this poll, I think.

Meanwhile, the next time I bung [toss] money to Amnesty International I'd like it to go towards some investigation into real human-rights abuses somewhere in the world, rather than towards a self-serving opinion poll which was designed to make some of us look like fools.

> "Victims argue that the church needs to take radical steps—not incremental ones—to create an environment that will protect children from predatory priests."

More Aggressive Actions by the Catholic Church Will Protect Children from Sexual Abuse by Clergy

Jane Lampman

In the following viewpoint, Jane Lampman describes how, after initial hesitation, the Catholic Church is making greater strides in addressing the sexual abuse of minors by priests. Though some dioceses have longstanding guidelines in place for dealing with offenders, many victims feel that more aggressive actions, including preventative measures, are needed, and churches in some areas are taking steps in that direction. Some of these steps include the prompt removal of offenders from ministry, implementation of clearer review procedures, and development of victim-outreach programs. Jane Lampman is a staff writer for the Christian Science Monitor.

As you read, consider the following questions:

1. What happened in the Boston area that represented a dramatic shift in the treatment of sexual abuse cases?
2. The article lists three things victims want in order to create a more protective environment for children within the church. What are they?
3. What was the outcome of Phil Saviano's court case against the priest who molested him?

Twice in the past month, Jim Sacco has been elated by the news. First, John Geoghan, the Boston-area priest who Mr. Sacco says molested him and his four siblings 35 years ago, was convicted of molesting another child and is in jail.

Then, the Boston Archdiocese began taking steps to prevent such abuse—after long ignoring victims' pleas to do so.

"This has been bothering me my whole life," says Sacco of Amherst, N.H., who no longer attends church. "The church has dealt with victims extremely poorly."

More than anyone, abuse victims and their families have felt the Roman Catholic Church's recalcitrance in better addressing sexual exploitation of young people by priests. Victims and their supporters have pressed the church for reforms, but say they've made little headway.

Now, as dioceses such as Los Angeles and Philadelphia announce reforms in the wake of the Boston scandal, victims like Sacco—who say they've seen previous scandals come and go with no real change in church actions—see glimmers of hope.

Most heartening to victims and their allies is a shift in public attitude in the Boston area that has forced the archdiocese to remove priests with a record of abuse, and to turn their names over to law-enforcement officials. That's a dramatic departure from the longstanding practice of handling such cases behind closed doors, with silence a condition of financial compensation for victims.

It's also the first time the debate has included calls for a church leader to resign—an effort to hold responsible not the pedophile but also officials who transferred him among parishes.

"That has been unthinkable," says A.W. Richard Sipe, a former priest turned therapist who has treated victims and accused clerics. "So this is monumental."

Scope of the Problem

To many who have been abused, serious consequences for engaging in or overlooking sexual exploitation represent the greatest hope for handling a problem that some say has grown over the years to include 3,000 priests and tens of thousands of victims. Still, both they and others are cautious in their expectations. Ten years ago, there was an outcry over the case of James Porter, a former priest sentenced to 18 to 20 years in Fall River, Mass., after more than 200 adults in several states said they were his victims.

Yet "nothing essentially changed since that last time around—they were still pulling these guys back into ministry and they were not dealing with the victims and their families," says Peter Isely, a therapist in Milwaukee, Wis., who in the past has run a victims' program. "The question is what is going to be different this time around."

Victims argue that the church needs to take radical steps— not incremental ones - to create an environment that will protect children from predatory priests. Among their desires: Clergy should be required to report allegations of abuse immediately to authorities and let them carry out the investigation. The church should remove the cleric and tell his parish why, so that parents can communicate with their children. And they want prevention programs that will educate the clergy about the problem and requirements to report abuse.

"More parents, police, prosecutors, and politicians need to show courage and . . . insist on the right steps," says David Clohessy, director of Survivors Network of Those Abused by Priests.

In some parts of the country, policies have been in place for at least a decade. The United States Conference of Catholic Bishops (USCCB), which coordinates Catholic activities and education, set up an ad hoc committee in 1993 that drew up guidelines for dioceses. Many of the 194 dioceses have written policies, and a few have victim-assistance programs.

"I'm not sure you can ever do enough for a victim, but the bishops have tried extensively for 15 years or more," says William Ryan, the USCCB's deputy director of communications. "I don't think there's been any issue the bishops have . . . dealt with more thoroughly."

Those dealing with victims see the situation differently. "I've been involved in 55 cases since 1993, and in almost all of them the church has resisted the allegations," Mr. Sipe says.

Jeff Anderson, a lawyer in St. Paul, Minn., who has handled more than 400 such cases, says the church sometimes plays hardball. Two years ago in Portland, Ore., for example, it served a countersuit on a victim at his place of business, charging his suit lacked merit. Forty-three other individuals came forward. A case on behalf of 23 was settled; a second is under way for 20.

Perceptions that the church is unresponsive leads many to sue. "The Catholic Church is acting like every other institution whose leaders are exposed for abuse—with self-protection," says the Rev. Patricia Liberty, director of Associates in Prevention and Education in Pastoral Practice, which works with clergy and victims across denominations. "Because they act like an institution instead of . . . a church, it adds another layer of pain. . . ." Victims turn to the courts, she adds, when the church fails to listen.

The Clergy Sexual Abuse Scandal's Hold on American Catholic Life is Loosening

- The number of clergy sex abuse claims received by the nation's Catholic bishops and religious orders declined in 2006. . . .

- A survey conducted in October 2005 found 74 percent of Catholics were either "somewhat" or "very" satisfied with U.S. bishops' leadership, up from 57 percent in January 2003, according to the Georgetown University Center for Applied Research in the Apostolate.

- The nation's pre-eminent victims' advocate group, the Survivors Network of those Abused by Priests, continues to press for reforms in the Roman Catholic Church but has expanded its lobbying efforts to Southern Baptists and other churches.

Eric Gorski,
World Wide Religious News,
July 11, 2007.

That was the case for Phil Saviano, who says he was molested by a young priest in his Massachusetts parish in the 1960s. Reading a 1992 article in the *Boston Globe* about Fr. David Holley abusing youngsters in New Mexico spurred him to tell his story. When the diocese responded that there had been no problems with Father Holley in Massachusetts, Mr. Saviano sued for the files.

"What I ended up with was . . . letters signed by bishops in four states and a vicar of priests in a fifth, outlining the times he was caught molesting kids, all the times he was sent to a treatment program, and moved to a new parish without the parishioners being warned," he says.

Holley was prosecuted in New Mexico and received the longest sentence ever given to a Catholic priest—275 years.

In the wake of the Boston revelations, Catholic bishops in Philadelphia and Los Angeles have said that no priest will be returned to parish ministry after a substantiated allegation of sexual abuse of minors. That was already the case in Chicago and Cleveland. In a survey of the 25 largest US dioceses, the *Boston Globe* found only those four cities (of 13 that responded) had written policies to that effect. Only five required clergy and employees to report allegations to police or child-welfare agencies. Many states do not require clergy to report abuse.

More Responsive Policies

Some dioceses have taken steps to set up clear review procedures and to reach out more to victims. Chicago's Cardinal Joseph Bernadin, once falsely accused of abuse, is credited by many for establishing a responsive approach. A decade ago, Chicago set up a board of lay people and clergy to handle allegations, and a separate office to help victims get counseling.

"If trust has been abused by a member of the church, it can be a difficult journey for people to come back and seek help from the church," says Ralph Bonaccorsi, director of the Chicago archdiocese's Office of Conciliation and Assistance Ministry. The archdiocese also sponsors an annual conference for staff in other dioceses who offer such services.

Mr. Bonaccorsi's office offers therapeutic and spiritual counseling for victims. When a priest is removed, he meets with local leaders and parishioners to discuss why, and to work toward healing.

Isely, the Milwaukee therapist, says Cardinal Bernadin met with victims and intended, before his death in 1996, to promote a public conversation with them.

The Archdiocese of Milwaukee was one of the first to do victim outreach when it initiated Project Benjamin back in

1989. "For many people, their first choice is that the church respond to them," says former director Elizabeth Piasecki. They develop individual care plans and pay for counseling. "We had no litigation after we established that process."

Others attribute that result to the church's success in getting the state supreme court to say it can't be sued in Wisconsin. "They make the claim in every state that it would infringe on free exercise of religion," says Mr. Anderson, the St. Paul lawyer. "But Wisconsin is the only place the high court has accepted that."

The High Cost of Inaction

It's not surprising that the church would seek to avoid litigation. A report from the US bishops conference in 1985 warned that it could cost the church $1 billion in the next decade unless it addressed the problem. Some say it has paid out that much, but the church says the amount is exaggerated.

Survivors say more than money, victims want to be believed, and to be sure that other kids will be protected. Financial settlements represent that acknowledgement. "I'd trade all the written and verbal apologies for one safe-touch program in all Catholic schools," says Mr. Clohessy of Survivors Network.

> "*[Catholics] do not [make donations]*
> *... to advance the cause of an organi-*
> *zation that appears determined to cover*
> *up criminal activity.*"

The Catholic Church
Covers Up Sexual Abuse
with Victim Payoffs

Donald P. Russo

While monetary settlement of child sexual abuse claims against the Catholic Church may compensate victims, it also helps church leaders avoid having to testify to the church's fifty-year cover up of these crimes, maintains Donald P. Russo in the following viewpoint. The church has for generations been giving comfort and support to clergy who are known to sexually abuse children, which is the crime for which monetary settlements are paying, he claims. Parishioners do not make donations to the church to fund the cover-up of criminal activity, Russo argues. Russo is a Bethlehem, Pennsylvania, attorney.

As you read, consider the following questions:

1. Why does Russo think the argument that parishioners are not paying for the monetary settlement of sexual abuse claims is a weak one?

2. What are the weapons of choice of one who sexually abuses children, according to the author?

3. What, in the author's opinion, is the "few bad eggs" defense?

Tradition is powerful in our lives. We continue following certain behaviors and routines because they are what we were taught to do. Catholics continue going to Mass on Sunday, despite overwhelming evidence that the church has been involved in some monstrous misdeeds. [In July 2007], the Roman Catholic Archdiocese of Los Angeles agreed to pay $660 million to 500 victims of sexual abuse dating back as far as the 1940s. It was the largest compensation of its kind ever recorded. The settlement means victims will receive more than $1 million each.

We are getting used to hearing about financial compensation being paid by the church to those who have been abused by priests. . . . The suit was filed by 12 plaintiffs who accused former priest Clinton Hagenbach of molesting them. Hagenbach died in the 1980s. Had the case gone to trial, lawyers would have been able to place Cardinal Roger Mahony, archbishop of Los Angeles, in the untenable position of having to testify about the church's cover-up of abuses dating from the 1940s to the 1990s. The *Los Angeles Times* has estimated that the Los Angeles Archdiocese has real estate holdings worth more than $4 billion. The archdiocese in Boston has also been involved in large settlement payouts for victims of sexual abuse. "Though it has always been the position of the Archdiocese that the insurance companies must honor their responsibility to fund a major share of future settlements, the Archdiocese must also be prepared to fund its share of these coming settlements," Cardinal Mahony said in a May [2007] statement.

Covering Up a Crime

According to the cardinal, "this will require the Archdiocese to begin to dispose of nonessential real estate properties in order to raise funds for coming settlements, and to reevaluate some of the services and ministries it provides to parishes." Basically, the archdiocese is attempting to argue that these settlement proceeds are not coming out of the weekly collection baskets of parishioners. That argument is a weak one. First, if there is enough cash on hand to make these settlements, one has to wonder why the Sunday collection basket is still being passed around so avidly. Parishioners who make donations to the church do so out of a desire to enhance the church's ability to do God's work on earth. They do not do so out of a desire to advance the cause of an organization that appears determined to cover up criminal activity. And, there is no doubt that the sexual abuse of a minor constitutes felonious conduct. Assisting in the cover-up of that activity is a crime, plain and simple. Covering up a crime or conspiring to cover up a crime makes one a conspirator.

I was raised as a Roman Catholic, but I have not been able to attend Mass for quite some time now. I find it hard to fathom the notion that Catholics are supposed to merely shrug their shoulders over acts that have been perpetrated by the clergy that were nothing short of monstrous. There is nothing worse than the sexual abuse of a child by an adult authority figure. Feelings of respect for authority and fear of adults on the part of the child serve as the weapon of choice for the abuser. The abuser easily has his way, because the child feels that it is his or her obligation to "obey." I shudder to think of what I would want to do to any member of the clergy who had abused any child of mine.

A Crime by Men of God

Yes, we have heard the "few bad eggs" defense from the church. In other words, we are to believe that these acts of child abuse are being perpetrated solely by a few, and therefore we should not judge the church harshly. But this is only where the wrongdoing begins. It is the cover-up of the activity that becomes the worst crime of all. Moreover, these acts are being perpetrated by men in collars who are supposed to be men of God.

The Catholic Church has a history of encouraging sexual repression, in the name of all that is good and holy. At the same time, however, it has harbored, succored and given comfort and support to sexual predators who have permanently destroyed thousands of young lives. The victims will continue to suffer until the day that they die. Despite all of this, and despite all the evidence that the Church has been running a child abuse cover-up cartel for generations, Catholics still flock to Mass every Sunday. While that is certainly every Catholic's choice to make, he or she must have to wonder where their monetary contributions are going.

> *"Rape victims . . . should be offered un-*
> *biased factual information regarding*
> *. . . emergency contraception."*

Hospitals Should Offer Emergency Contraception to Rape Victims

Erin Varner

Hospitals should provide rape victims with unbiased information about emergency contraception so that they can make informed medical decisions, argues Erin Varner in the following viewpoint. When hospital personnel force their own moral judgments upon rape victims by refusing to provide them with information on emergency contraception, they further traumatize these victims, Varner claims. Hospitals should treat rape victims with the same level of care as other crime victims by providing them with all the tools available to help them heal, she maintains. Varner is a domestic violence crisis center advocate in Allegheny County, Pennsylvania.

As you read, consider the following questions:

1. To what is Varner exposed that many state legislators and community members never hear or read about?

Erin Varner, "Rape Victims Deserve the Best of Care," *Pittsburgh Post-Gazette*, July 18, 2007. www.post-gazette.com. Reproduced by permission of the author.

2. What issue may not be addressed if the option to take emergency contraception is not presented to rape victims, in the author's view?

3. Why do some medical professionals choose to withhold information about emergency contraception, in the author's opinion?

A rapist usually is not a shadowed, unrecognizable figure, but rather, in most cases, a person his victim knows and may love. The Family Violence Prevention Fund reports that 76 percent of rape victims 18 and over knew their attacker. Often he was a current or former spouse, a partner, a date.

As a victims' advocate for a domestic-violence agency, I am exposed daily to cases that state legislators and community members never hear or read about. A woman victimized by her boyfriend and his buddies after going on a drug binge. A teenage girl, on her first date, raped on a couch at a party. A woman forced to engage in "makeup sex" after her husband beat her.

The Treatment of Rape Victims

Rape is a brutal demonstration of one's power and control over another person. It is frequently employed as a form of domestic abuse. As advocates, community members or legislators, we have an ethical, legal and moral obligation to help rape victims heal by using all of the medical, psychological and legal tools we have to restore their health and dignity.

When victims of any other crimes are injured, they receive the highest standard of care available when brought into a hospital. Gun shot, stabbing and choking wounds are surgically repaired, bandaged and the patient is provided with follow-up care. Victims of rape are not guaranteed the highest standard of care.

When entering a hospital for treatment, rape victims not only must deal with the physical trauma of their injuries, they

Emergency Contraception Is Not Abortion

Plan B, also called "the morning-after pill," does not cause abortions.

An abortion is the destruction/removal of a fertilized egg. Emergency contraception averts pregnancy by preventing fertilization—either by stopping the release of an egg or by making it difficult or impossible for sperm to penetrate the egg.

York (PA) Daily Record,
July 8, 2007.

also must battle the social stigma and personal moral judgments of those who care for them. A rape victim should clearly and compassionately be presented with choices as to whether they want to press charges, allow a rape kit investigation to be performed, speak with a victim's advocate or take drugs to prevent sexually transmitted infections.

Rape victims also should be offered unbiased factual information regarding the use and availability of emergency contraception. Unfortunately the option to take emergency contraception is not always presented, which means the issue of an unwanted pregnancy resulting from this violent crime may or may not be addressed.

A study done in 2006 by the ACLU [American Civil Liberties Union] Clara Bell Reproductive Freedom Project showed that only 47 percent of Pennsylvania hospitals offer emergency contraception to rape victims. This means that in the majority of Pennsylvania hospitals, women are not being told that emergency contraception might allow them to avoid the devastating consequence of a pregnancy resulting from rape.

Every victim has a right to the same standard of care when seeking treatment after a rape, a right that would be ensured by . . . legislation [that] would mandate that a rape victim be informed of the availability of emergency contraception in an objective manner by a medical professional. Victims have a right to make informed medical decisions for themselves, based on their own situations, beliefs and complete information about their options.

At the moment, more than half of Pennsylvania hospitals deny women the right to choose emergency contraception even though many women who have been raped do not know that it is available.

As residents of a metropolitan area, we may take for granted that we have easy access to a number of different hospitals. But even in cities, some hospitals do not tell rape victims about emergency contraception and, even in those that do, some medical professionals choose to withhold information about emergency contraception due to their personal moral convictions. And even with all of our choices as city residents, a woman rendered unconscious as a result of an attack is unable to choose which hospital she is taken to.

This problem is all the more prevalent in rural areas, where the only hospital accessible to a rape victim might choose to keep her in the dark about the availability of emergency contraception.

Shouldn't all rape victims be presented with the same options and information so they can make informed decisions? Shouldn't all rape victims have the opportunity to make decisions about their own medical treatment? How do we ethically deny some women the care that others receive?

One in five women will become a victim of rape. If tomorrow someone you love becomes a part of this statistic, wouldn't you want to know that she will be told about all of her medical options?

> "A child conceived in rape is a human being and deserves legal protection despite the horrific circumstances of conception."

Hospitals Should Not Offer Emergency Contraception to Rape Victims

Matt Sande

Hospitals and personnel who oppose abortion should not be forced to offer emergency contraception to rape victims, asserts Matt Sande in the following viewpoint. Since human life begins at fertilization, any artificial action that deliberately destroys the fertilized egg is an abortion, he maintains. Since one of the ways emergency contraception works it to prevent the fertilized egg from implanting in the womb, Sande contends that it is a chemical abortion that destroys a human life. Despite the horror of rape, he argues, the child conceived is a human being that should be protected. Sande is director of legislation for Pro-Life Wisconsin.

Matt Sande, "Testimony In Opposition to SB 129/AB 377: 'Emergency Contraception' Hospital Mandate, Assembly Committee on Judiciary and Ethics" Pro-Life Wisconsin, September 6, 2007.

As you read, consider the following questions:

1. In Sande's view, how can emergency contraception harm women?

2. What is the problem with a standard pregnancy test, according to the author?

3. In the author's opinion, how does the U.S. Constitution protect the right of hospitals to refuse to participate in morally objectionable practices?

Good morning Chairman Gundrum and Committee members. My name is Matt Sande and I serve as director of legislation for Pro-Life Wisconsin. Thank you for this opportunity to speak against Senate Bill (SB) 129 / Assembly Bill (AB) 377, legislation mandating all Wisconsin hospitals, regardless of religious affiliation, inform an alleged victim of sexual assault about "emergency contraception" and provide it upon her request.

Our primary opposition to this legislation is based on the abortion-causing action of so-called "emergency contraception." Emergency contraception (EC), also known as the 'morning-after' pill, is basically two high doses of the birth control pill taken within a 72-hour period. It can work in three ways: to suppress ovulation; to inhibit the mobility of sperm, and to alter the lining of the uterus so that a newly conceived child is unable to implant in the womb, thus starving and dying. This last action is pre-implantation chemical abortion.

The most commonly used emergency contraceptive pill package is Plan B. The website for this drug regimen clearly indicates that it can work to prevent a fertilized egg from implanting in the uterine wall:

Source: www.go2planb.com under "What is Plan B®" then go to "How Plan B® Works:" Plan B® works like a regular birth control pill. It prevents pregnancy mainly by stopping the

125

release of an egg from the ovary, and may also prevent the fertilization of an egg (the uniting of sperm with the egg). *Plan B® may also work by preventing it [fertilized egg] from attaching to the uterus (womb) (emphasis added).* It is important to know that Plan B® will not affect a fertilized egg already attached to the uterus; it will not affect an existing pregnancy.

As indicated above, the makers of Plan B contend that emergency contraception does not cause an abortion. They argue that emergency contraception prevents pregnancy and thereby reduces the need for induced abortion. However, they intentionally define the term "pregnancy" as *implantation* of a fertilized egg in the lining of a woman's uterus, as opposed to "pregnancy" beginning at *fertilization*. Whether one understands pregnancy as beginning at "implantation" or "fertilization" makes no difference; the heart of the matter is when human life begins. Embryological science has clearly determined that human life begins at fertilization—the fusion of an egg and sperm immediately resulting in a new, genetically distinct human being. This is not a subjective opinion, but an objective scientific fact. Accordingly, any artificial action that works to destroy a fertilized egg (human embryo) is abortifacient in nature.

Not only can EC kill a tiny preborn life in its earliest stages, but it can also harm women. Plan B is associated with blood clot formation and a heightened risk of ectopic pregnancy. The common side-effects of the 'morning-after pill' (nausea and abdominal pain) are also the symptoms of an ectopic pregnancy and could therefore mask the presence of this potentially life-threatening condition. Importantly, there are no long-term studies to show whether women will be permanently damaged, or risk such diseases as cancer, from these chemicals being given in such high doses. Forcing physicians to immediately provide medication to patients based solely upon their request is simply bad medicine. In the case of

An Online Catholic Community's Beliefs on Emergency Contraception

Would you want emergency contraception if you, your wife or daughter were raped?

Yes, I would not hesitate at all. The thought of bearing a rapist's child sounds like it would add to the trauma.	36	12.00%
I would strongly consider it after consulting with a priest.	13	4.33%
I would probably hesitate because of fear of preventing the implantation of a fertilized egg.	9	3.00%
I would never, under any circumstances, use artificial birth control. If a child were born, I would surrender it for adoption.	72	24.00%
I would never try and prevent the birth of any baby. I would raise the child myself.	112	37.33%
This is a difficult question. I don't know what I'd do or how I'd feel in that circumstance.	47	15.67%
Other	11	3.67%

TAKEN FROM: Catholic Answers, May 2005.

emergency contraception, such a policy may contradict a physician's medical judgment as EC could be medically contraindicated for the patient.

Planned Parenthood of Wisconsin has argued that the Ethical and Religious Directives (ERDs) for Catholic Health Care Services "make clear that EC is an acceptable treatment option for rape victims who are not pregnant." This statement is vague at best, especially considering Planned Parenthood's understanding of pregnancy as implantation. ERD #36 states:

> "A female who has been raped should be able to defend herself against a potential conception from the sexual assault. If, after appropriate testing, there is no evidence that conception has occurred already, she may be treated with medications that would prevent ovulation, sperm capacitation, or fertilization. It is not permissible, however, to initiate or to recommend treatments that have as their purpose or direct effect the removal, destruction, or interference with the implantation of a fertilized ovum (emphasis added)."

Pro-Life Wisconsin sympathizes with victims of sexual assault. It is impossible, however, to determine whether or not fertilization has occurred at the time EC is directed to be taken. Although SB 129 does not require a hospital "to provide emergency contraception to a victim who is pregnant, as indicated by a test for pregnancy," a standard pregnancy test cannot accurately determine fertilization nor is it designed to do so. Standard pregnancy tests only determine implantation. The bill does not define the term "pregnancy," and it is uncertain how DHFS would interpret the statutory language in promulgating rules, enforcing noncompliance, and assessing forfeitures. The situation can be likened to a hunter who sees something moving in the bushes and holds his fire until he is sure that it is not a person. We must act with the same restraint in protecting newly conceived human life.

For this reason and others, the Vatican's Pontifical Academy for Life has publicly opposed the use of the morning-after pill for *any* reason. At its Annual Meeting in 2003, the Catholic Medical Association passed a resolution stating that the term 'emergency contraception' is a misnomer as it does not consistently prevent fertilization. The resolution concludes that the drug "has the potential to prevent implantation whether given in the pre-ovulatory, ovulatory, or post-ovulatory phase, that it cannot be ethically employed by a Catholic physician or administered in a Catholic hospital in cases of rape."

Furthermore, Wisconsin law protects the right of hospitals to refuse to participate in morally objectionable practices such as abortion and sterilization. The proposed legislation appears to be in conflict with Wisconsin Statutes 253.09(1) because of the abortion causing effect of so-called emergency contraceptive drugs, as well as with the Wisconsin Constitution which expressly protects the rights of conscience. Under Article 1, Section 18 of our state constitution "any control of, or interference with, the rights of conscience" shall not be permitted. The bill also violates the First Amendment to the United States Constitution which guarantees the right to freely exercise one's religious convictions. These conscience rights are enshrined in our state law, state constitution, and federal constitution for good reason—to secure liberty in a free nation.

A truly "pro-choice" position would defend the right of hospitals and health care workers to refuse to participate in the ending of a newly-formed human life, SB 129/AB 377 is a government mandate that forces places of healing to become places where a sexual assault victim is not offered genuine compassion, but a pill that could end life of an innocent person—something additional to weigh on her mind and emotions.

A child conceived in rape is a human being and deserves legal protection despite the horrific circumstance of conception. The personhood of a child is not contingent upon the circumstances surrounding his or her conception. We need to offer compassion to all the innocent parties in a sexual assault. Assisting rape victims who want to place their children for adoption, advocating counseling programs for victims and providing financial, material and moral support for mothers who decide to keep their children is the truly compassionate response.

LIFE BEGINS AT FERTILZATION. SB 129/AB 377 is anti-life, anti-choice, and undemocratic. It is an abortion bill and those who vote for it are forcing chemical abortion on our state's hospitals. I urge the Committee to vote NO on SB 129/AB 377. Thank you for your consideration.

Periodical Bibliography

The following articles have been selected to supplement the diverse views presented in this chapter.

America	"Sin and Scandal," November 26, 2007.
Victoria A. Brownworth	"Fighting Rape on Campus," *Curve*, April 2006.
Jo Carlowe	"Behind the Headlines: Can Emergency Pill Stem Abortion?" *GP*, September 29, 2006.
Boston University Daily Free Press	"Offer Pill to Rape Victims," April 14, 2005.
Economist	"Slow Progress; Tackling Rape," November 17, 2007.
Eric Gorski	"Catholic Abuse Crisis Starts to Fade," *World-Wide Religious News*, July 11, 2007.
Drew Haugen	"Sexual Violence Affects Everyone," *Rocky Mountain Collegian*, March 2, 2006.
Peter Katel	"Future of the Catholic Church," *CQ Researcher*, January 19, 2007.
Anne Kingston	"Ever Hear the One About the Chick Who Got Raped? We Know Rape Is Serious. So How Did It Become the Joke du Jour?" *MacLean's*, July 9, 2007.
Rita Larivee	"Our Greatest Responsibility," *National Catholic Reporter*, November 16, 2007.
Victoria Lucia	"Banned from Buying Emergency Contraception. It Could Happen to You," *Cosmopolitan*, August 2007.
York (PA) Daily Record	"Make Plan B Available," July 8, 2007.

OPPOSING
VIEWPOINTS®
SERIES

CHAPTER 4

What Policies Will Help Reduce Sexual Violence?

Chapter Preface

Highly publicized cases of sexual violence so outrage the public conscience that policy makers often feel compelled to take strong action and quickly. Civil libertarians claim, however, that such hastily crafted laws rarely create an effective balance between the need to punish and prevent crime and the corresponding need to protect individual liberty. The debate over civil commitment laws reflects this tension between the need to protect the public while also protecting civil liberties. After the abduction, rape, and murder of nineteen-year-old Kansas college student Stephanie Schmidt by a repeat sex offender, Kansas enacted a sex offender law that included civil commitment. Civil commitment laws confine sexually violent criminals that have been judged a continued danger to others after they have completed their prison sentence.

Proponents of civil commitment maintain that such laws protect society from dangerous sexual predators by isolating them from society. According to New York state senator Joseph Bruno, "[Civil commitment] legislation will save lives, protect our children and keep our communities safe by making sure dangerous sexual predators are kept off the streets." Supporters also refute the claim that civil commitment laws are a slippery slope to a police state. According to Joe Diamond, founder of Take Back New York, an influential grassroots anticrime group, "In the abstract, infringing on the liberties of law-breakers may threaten 'everyone.' But in the real world, it actually saves lives." Enacting laws that restrict the lives of criminals to protect the innocent "doesn't mean we are becoming a totalitarian society," he maintains. "If anything it means we are returning to the days . . . when society drew clear lines between right and wrong," Diamond reasons.

Opponents of civil commitment contend that such laws sacrifice constitutionally protected freedoms. They claim, for example, that civil commitment laws are too broad and therefore punish sex offenders who are not a danger to the public. Enacted in reaction to highly publicized but rare crimes, "sexually violent predator laws conflate physical violence with consensual sex with teenagers, casting a wider net than its name implies," asserts writer and activist Mark McHarry. Moreover, opponents argue, the laws have not psychiatrically defined the diagnosis for which a convicted sexual predator will be committed. Critics say that lawmakers, not doctors, create these diagnoses, which are so vague that they could apply to millions of people. Many psychiatric organizations see these civil commitment laws "as unethical incarceration of the non-mentally ill," McHarry maintains. In addition, opponents observe, civil commitment laws are written as civil law and do not have the constitutionally protected safeguards of criminal law. "Fundamental constitutional protections are weakened or absent, notably double jeopardy (repeated punishment for the same crime) . . . and ex post facto (prohibiting a punitive measure created after a crime has been committed)," McHarry explains. "Because the predator laws apply only to a personality disorder and because they lack the safeguards of criminal law, they give state legislatures the ability to extend indefinite confinement to any other behavior lawmakers consider deviant or delinquent," McHarry reasons.

Whether civil commitment adequately strikes the balance between protecting the public and safeguarding civil liberties is reflective of other debates concerning what policies will help reduce sexual violence. The authors in the following chapter debate some of these other hotly contested policies.

| "In order for prosecutors to have the tools they need, there must be strong [sex offender] laws at both the federal and state level."

Strict Sex Offender Laws Will Reduce Sexual Violence

Alberto R. Gonzales

The strictest penalties possible are necessary to protect America's children from pedophiles and sexual predators, argues former U.S. attorney general Alberto R. Gonzales in the following viewpoint taken from a speech to the national convention of state legislatures. To get sex offenders off the streets, he maintains, all U.S. states should adopt harsh mandatory minimum sentences. To prevent pornographers from abusing children, states should criminalize all child pornography offenses, he asserts. Moreover, Gonzales claims, states should consider civil commitment of dangerous sexual predators to remove the threat they pose.

As you read, consider the following questions:

1. What does Gonzales want U.S. prosecutors to show the world?

Alberto R. Gonzales, "Prepared Remarks of Attorney General Alberto R. Gonzales to the National Conference of State Legislatures," December 8, 2006. www.usdoj.gov/ag.

2. What tools do prosecutors need to keep pedophiles and predators behind bars, in the author's view?

3. How many jurisdictions does the author assert have no mandatory minimum sentences for those convicted of pornography offenses?

A child's innocence is under siege every day from images, sounds, movies and music. And by far, the greatest threat is the one posed by pedophiles and sexual predators. We must do all that we can to protect our children from these cowardly villains who hide in the shadows of the Internet.

I know that you are already doing a lot in your states to safeguard the innocence of our children. Many of you have been leaders in the fight against online predators and in creating sex offender registries to help keep your communities safe. For that I want to say thank you, and God bless you.

But more can be done.

Marshaling Resources

That's why in February of [2006] I announced Project Safe Childhood, a Justice Department initiative aimed at ending abuse and exploitation of kids through the internet. Project Safe Childhood marshals the efforts of law enforcement at the federal, state, and local level, along with non-governmental organizations, so that we can make the best use of our resources and obtain the toughest penalties possible under the law. . . .

Please join me, and each other, in building a national, zero-tolerance attitude towards pedophiles and sexual predators.

As a society, we already share a revulsion for what these criminals do to our children. But if we are to really stop pedophiles and predators before they strike . . . we need to move our country past revulsion, on to determination fueled by outrage, and finally on to action by parents, community organizations, legislators and law enforcement.

Getting Predators Off the Streets

First, to put it in the simplest of terms, we need to get pedophiles and predators off the streets.

I told prosecutors that they need to be aggressive in the cases they bring—to show the world that there is no gray area when it comes to hurting kids.

I have asked law enforcement to discipline themselves so that no lead will ever cross the threshold of a prosecutor's office, local police precinct or advocacy center without some kind of follow-up and action. If there is evidence that a child has been hurt, I want to see an arrest, a thorough investigation, and a merciless prosecution if we have the evidence.

As leaders in your States, you have the power to improve investigations, to get pedophiles and predators off the streets by reviewing your computer forensic capabilities and ensuring that they are up-to-speed for dealing with the criminals who target our children, as well as other offenders who use the Internet to facilitate their crimes. We cannot allow ourselves to be "outgunned" by criminals whose knowledge of the Internet and computers exceeds our own. I urge all of you to make sure you build the necessary computer forensic capacity for your law enforcement agencies.

Keeping Predators Behind Bars

Second, once we get them off the street, we need to keep the pedophiles and predators behind bars.

This is an area where you as legislators can make a unique contribution to our partnership. We must have stiff state-level penalties for these criminals. I've told law enforcement that where state laws are more aggressive, it should be a state-level case. If the federal law will put a pedophile behind bars for longer, it should be a federal case.

But in order for prosecutors to have the tools they need, there must be strong laws at both the federal and state level. State and local prosecutors far outnumber those at the federal level, and they must be empowered to fully join in this fight. Many of you here today have done an outstanding job on this point, and I want to commend you for that.

But there are still two states that do not criminalize possession of child pornography without intent to distribute. In six states it is possible for someone to be convicted of possession as only a misdemeanor.

While most states' child pornography laws consider persons under age 18 to be minors, five jurisdictions continue to set the age limit at 17, and five others set it at only 16.

And 20 jurisdictions do not provide mandatory minimum sentences for those convicted of production, distribution, or possession with intent to distribute child pornography.

As a former State government official myself, I can assure you that nobody is more willing than I am to acknowledge that our great national experiment in Democracy and Federalism requires us to celebrate our diversity of laws. But there are some things I think we can agree on, including that perpetrators of these vile crimes should face some minimum sentence. I am not here to tell you exactly what that minimum should be; that's for you to decide.

The National Consensus

And again, many of you have already had that debate and adopted minimum sentences. I only respectfully, and I repeat, respectfully, ask those states that have not taken action to join the national consensus of setting some meaningful floor in sentencing these criminals. There should not be any place in this country where a judge could let a child sex offender go free with nothing more than probation. There should not be any jurisdiction where predators can hide behind weak laws.

So experiment with the precise contours of your own laws—and maybe we all will learn from you. But I submit that no State in our Nation can do its duty by its kids unless it has protective laws with real teeth.

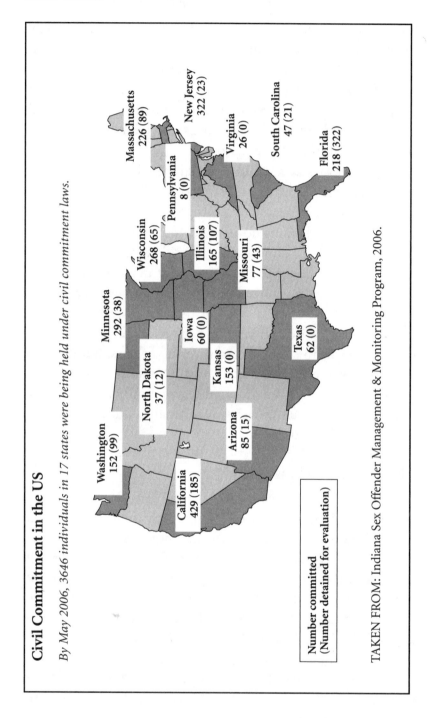

Civil Commitment in the US

By May 2006, 3646 individuals in 17 states were being held under civil commitment laws.

Washington
152 (99)

California
429 (185)

Arizona
85 (15)

North Dakota
37 (12)

Minnesota
292 (38)

Iowa
60 (0)

Kansas
153 (0)

Texas
62 (0)

Wisconsin
268 (65)

Illinois
165 (107)

Missouri
77 (43)

Pennsylvania
8 (0)

Massachusetts
226 (89)

New Jersey
322 (23)

Virginia
26 (0)

South Carolina
47 (21)

Florida
218 (322)

Number committed
(Number detained for evaluation)

TAKEN FROM: Indiana Sex Offender Management & Monitoring Program, 2006.

On our end, the Department of Justice is determined to step up with funding and assistance to equip law enforcement with all the knowledge they need so that they can work their cases.

I also support new regulations for the federal Bureau of Prisons to pursue the civil commitment of mentally abnormal or disordered sex offenders who would pose a serious danger to others if released. Congress has been creative; under the Adam Walsh Act they've given us the right to pursue that path and others like it, and we are going to.

For those of you who have done so much to protect children, civil commitment laws are another area you might consider in your states as a way of keeping dangerous offenders from re-offending . . . by continuing to incapacitate them, and by providing them treatment.

Zero-Tolerance

The third, and potentially most important step we all need to take to achieve zero-tolerance is old-fashioned communication—raising our voices, together, to raise awareness and teach prevention.

When he talked about the importance of the civil rights movement, the Reverend Martin Luther King, Junior, said that "History will have to record that the greatest tragedy of this period of social transition was not the strident clamor of the bad people, but the appalling silence of the good people."

That is still true today. For us to be silent on this issue is to fall short of our responsibilities as leaders in a battle to protect society's most vulnerable: our children. . . .

People often ask me what keeps me up at night. Obviously the threat of a terrorist attack never leaves my mind, and it is the top priority of our government to keep that from happening.

But it is the faces of child victims that haunt my dreams. I can see their eyes, that awful emptiness, as if their tiny souls are trying to detach themselves from their desecrated bodies. The images of these victims have become part of my heart, and I am not going to tire in this fight to protect them. . . .

I think there are some basic principles on which we should be unified, and I would ask all states to achieve these three things:

- Criminalize as a felony all child pornography offenses.

- Adopt harsher sentences and mandatory minimums.

- And set the definition of a "child" at 18 years.

And for those of you whose laws already do all that and more, I suggest you look for other creative opportunities to advance our cause. Work to develop digital forensics capacity in your State labs. Consider the option of civil commitment for dangerous sexual predators. Hit child pornographers in their wallets by requiring restitution for their victims.

I know you join me in looking forward to the day when we are routinely catching and prosecuting the criminal who is buying child pornography and has signed up to be a summer camp counselor . . . but hasn't yet touched a child.

A day when justice is served before an abusive parent invites his daughter's friends over for a slumber party.

A day when we never hear from the people who brag on the Internet about being revolutionaries, fighting for the so-called "sexual rights of children"—as though they are doing kids a favor by sexually molesting and exploiting them.

I want these pedophiles off the streets.

I want them put away for as long as the law will allow.

And I want all of society to act as one united front against this threat.

"Emotionally driven laws that not only punish sex offenders but also push them to the edges of society are counter-productive."

Strict Sex Offender Laws Will Not Reduce Sexual Violence

America

Strict laws that attempt to contain sex offenders who have served their sentences will not protect victims of sexual violence, claim the editors of America *in the following viewpoint. In fact, sex offenders who have been caught and punished have a low recidivism rate, the authors assert. The real threat of sexual violence comes not from strangers, but from friends and family, they maintain. Moreover, the authors argue, strict residency restrictions can lead to homelessness for perpetrators and vigilantism on the part of citizens, punishing people for crimes that they have not yet committed.* America *is a Roman Catholic national weekly published by the Society of Jesus.*

As you read, consider the following questions:

1. What does Jerome G. Miller claim has arisen because of civil commitment laws, as cited by *America*?

2. What types of sex offender laws can lead to homelessness, in the authors' view?

3. What do researchers at the National Center on Institutions and Alternatives claim will reduce the number of
   victims of sex offenders?

Civil commitment is a sanitized term for statutes that keep
sex offenders behind bars long after they have served
their prison sentences. Indefinite commitment laws of this
kind have been rapidly increasing around the country, and
thousands of people are being held far beyond their actual
terms. As sure-fire vote-getters in the wake of a handful of
high-profile sexual abuse murders, such laws are to a large extent politically driven, with little thought given to unjust consequences. The latest such law, the 20th, was passed in New
York. Governor Eliot Spitzer signed legislation in mid-March
[2007] that he claims will become a national model.

Civil Incarceration

Civil rights and prisoners' rights advocates correctly point out,
however, that civil commitment legislation incarcerates a person not only for crimes he has committed, but also because of
crimes he might commit. What is often overlooked, too, is the
fact that the vast majority of child molesters are not strangers,
but relatives or family friends of the victims. And contrary to
popular belief, once-caught sex offenders have a very low recidivism rate. The Bureau of Justice Statistics found in a three-
year study (2001–4) that only 5.3 percent of people arrested
for sex crimes were rearrested for a later sex offense.

The U.S. Supreme Court approved the constitutionality of
the indefinite detention of sex offenders in a case brought in
1997 in Kansas, so long as they receive treatment. And skilled
treatment can indeed be effective in reducing recidivism rates.
According to researchers at the National Center on Institutions and Alternatives, reliable studies indicate that high qual-

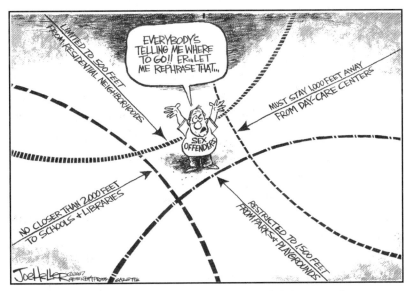

ity programs do work. But in some facilities to which offenders are sent after completing their prison sentences, the treatment may be of poor quality, administered by minimally trained therapists. According to Jerome G. Miller, co-founder of the National Center on Institutions and Alternatives and himself a therapist, civil commitment laws have "birthed a therapy industry."

Legal Restrictions

Even if sex offenders do not remain physically confined after completing their sentences, their lives are so constrained by residency restrictions that homelessness becomes a real possibility. There are laws that prohibit them from living within a certain distance of schools, playgrounds or other places where children gather. Registries of sex offenders now exist online, with close to three-quarters of a million names. Mandated community notification may include the circulation of flyers with photos of released offenders, which can make it impossible for ex-offenders to find a place to live.

Miami offers an extreme example of the lengths to which residency restrictions can go. Aware of the inability of a group of released offenders to find housing in communities reluctant to accept them, the state's corrections department finally allowed the men to live below a Biscayne Bay causeway. Their belongings in plastic bags, they sleep on mats on the pavement, with the rumble of cars overhead. The Miami situation, Dr. Miller told *America*, is a sign of where the laws are leading: taking residency restrictions policies to an extreme.

The danger of harassment and vigilantism becomes all the more likely too. The homes of released offenders have been shot at and even set on fire, in order to drive them away. Vigilantism can lead to murder. In April of 2006, two released offenders were shot dead in Maine. Both were listed in sex-offender registries with their names and addresses. One victim was a man who, at 17, had a relationship with his 15-year-old girlfriend. A legislative proposal in Ohio would require convicted sex offenders to have green florescent license plates on their cars. Such tactics would surely attract harassment or even violence, and be tantamount to a modern form of the scarlet letter.[1]

Counterproductive Laws

Emotionally driven laws that not only punish sex offenders but also push them to the edges of society are counterproductive. Researchers at the National Center on Institutions and Alternatives point out that "if we truly want fewer victims, the focus must be shifted from more and more punishment to the actual funding of treatment programs," as well as research. Fred S. Berlin, M.D., founder and executive director of the Johns Hopkins Sexual Disorder clinic in Baltimore, Md., has observed that the issue is not solely one of criminal justice, but also a public health matter, an aspect of the situ-

1. The reference is to a Puritan punishment of colonial times in which an adulterer had to wear a large scarlet letter "A" on his or her chest.

tion that is largely overlooked. It is time to stem the rush to enact more demonizing laws that are both unjust and irresponsible, stemming as they do from extreme cases that hold the popular imagination in thrall.

> "[Rape shield] laws were enacted ... to encourage rape victims to come forward without fear."

Rape Shield Laws Are Intended to Protect Victims

Gloria Allred and Margery Somers

Rape shield laws that prohibit a rape victim's prior sexual conduct from being admitted as evidence are necessary to encourage women to report rapes, maintain Gloria Allred and Margery Somers in the following viewpoint. Unfortunately, rape shield laws vary widely from state to state, the authors note. Some include exceptions and judicial discretion that prevent these laws from acting as a shield for victims, Allred and Somers assert. To encourage women to bring rapists to justice, the authors argue, rape shield laws must be applied consistently. Allred is a partner and Somers an associate with the law firm Allred, Maroko & Goldberg.

As you read, consider the following questions:

1. According to Allred and Somers, why are rape shield laws that grant broad judicial discretion ineffective?

2. How did the New Jersey Supreme Court weaken its state's rape shield law, in the authors' opinion?

3. In the authors' view, where is the character of many rape victims still being assassinated?

Question: If there's a rape shield law in Colorado—and there is—why do we know so much about the sex life and mental health of the woman the prosecution alleges was a rape victim of basketball star Kobe Bryant?[1]

Rape shield laws, which every U.S. state has on its books, are designed to prohibit the alleged victim's prior sexual conduct from being admitted at trial. These laws were enacted over the past 30 years in order to encourage rape victims to come forward without fear that their private lives would be invaded. They were also designed to prevent jurors from wrongly concluding that a woman's prior sexual behavior was relevant to whether or not she had been raped. There's even a federal rape shield law, Rule 412 of the Federal Rules of Evidence, enacted in 1978.

But even the best efforts of victims' advocates have not made rape shield laws fully protective of rape survivors.

A Variety of Rape Shield Laws

Rape shield laws vary significantly, and offer numerous exceptions. Defense attorneys routinely broadcast information on victims' sex lives. Inconsistently applied, rape shield laws often do far too little to protect a victim's privacy, reputation and character. According to a 2002 analysis by George Washington University law professor Michelle Anderson, states have come up with four different types of rape shield laws:

- Twenty-five states have exceptions to their rape shield laws that may allow evidence of prior sexual conduct

1. The criminal rape case was dropped on September 1, 2004, after his alleged victim's sexual history was revealed in court. The civil case against Bryant was settled on March 1, 2005.

between the complainant and the accused, or evidence of an alternative source for a victim's injuries or for semen found on her. Still others allow evidence of a pattern of prior sexual conduct by the complainant, evidence of bias or motive to fabricate the sexual assault or evidence of prior false accusations by the complainant.

- Twelve states and the District of Columbia have laws that allow even further intrusion into the victim's past behavior. Modeled after Federal Rule 412, they allow at least one legislated exception, but also an additional exception based on the federal Constitution. An alleged victim's prior conduct can thus be admitted if a judge determines that such an admission is constitutionally required.

- Nine states, including Colorado, grant the judge the broad discretion to admit or bar evidence of a woman's sexual history. This discretion is exactly what was granted to judges before rape shield laws came into effect, so they don't function as shields at all.

- The remaining four states base their exceptions only on the relevance and purpose for which the evidence is offered.

Inconsistent Application

Even within these four categories, courts are inconsistent in their application of the law, and some rape shield laws have been challenged in court: In a Massachusetts case, rape defendants were granted access to a victim's psychiatric records, including conversations she had with rape crisis counselors. In July 2003 decision, New Jersey's Supreme Court weakened the state's strong rape shield law by allowing testimony about an alleged victim's prior sexual relationship with the accused.

Rape Shield Laws

States that have "rape shield laws," which prohibit the introduction of evidence about an accuser's sexual history or reputation [as of June 2004]	49
Year that a rape shield provision was enshrined in the Federal Rules of Evidence governing federal legal proceedings	1978
Poll respondents who think it is fair for (Kobe) Bryant's defense attorneys to discuss in court his accuser's sex life	46%
Respondents who think it is foul play for Bryant's defense to discuss his accuser's sex life	38%

TAKEN FROM: "Rape Shield Laws," *Issues and Controversies,*
June 11, 2004.

(Those in favor of stricter rape shield laws would argue that "no" still means "no," whether the victim had once allowed intimacies or not.)

Colorado's rape shield law should protect the alleged victim in the Kobe Bryant case, but before the trial even started, Pamela Mackey, Bryant's attorney, asked a witness whether the 19-year-old complaining witness's injuries were consistent with "a woman who had had sex with three different men in three different days?" Bryant's attorneys also have sought to admit evidence of the woman's medical and mental histories, revealed the alleged victim's name in court and even challenged the constitutionality of Colorado's rape shield law. (In what may be a case of closing the barn door after the horse got out, two Colorado state legislators then proposed tightening the state's rape shield law in order to better protect a victim's identity.)

Although rape shield laws attempt to protect an alleged victim's reputation and prevent her past sexual behavior from becoming an issue, character assassinations continue in the courtroom and, even more so, in the court of public opinion.

If rape shield laws are truly going to shield victims, they need to be applied consistently and with minimal exception. Justice will be served when the law can assure that a woman need not be afraid to come forward for fear of an assault on her character after she's already faced an assault on her body.

> *"Courts have to walk a fine line between allowing complainants to be smeared and preventing defendants from fully confronting the witnesses against them."*

Rape Shield Laws May Deny Justice to Defendants

Cathy Young

An accused rapist should be able to defend himself against his accuser, argues Cathy Young in the following viewpoint. While smearing the name of rape victims is reprehensible, if a woman has a history of making false claims of sexual assault, that fact is clearly relevant to defend against a claim of rape, Young asserts. If courts are increasingly willing to pursue rape claims with little corroborating evidence, the need to protect the defendant's right to confront his accuser with relevant evidence is even greater. Young is a contributing editor with Reason, *a libertarian news and commentary magazine.*

As you read, consider the following questions:

1. What does sexual assault activist Cynthia Stone claim is a standard tactic for rape defendants, according to the author?

Cathy Young, "Kobe's Rights," *Reason*, January 2004. www.reason.com. Reproduced by permission.

2. Why, in Young's view, is excluding all evidence of a woman's past sexual activity not as cut-and-dried an issue as it seems?

3. In the author's opinion, what is the fine line courts must walk in rape cases?

Kobe Bryant's alleged sexual assault has generated the usual media circus that follows criminal charges against professional athletes, especially for sex crimes. But even with all its tawdry details, the case raises some serious issues about the way the justice system treats rape complainants and defendants.

Bryant, [who in 2004 was a] 25-year-old Los Angeles Lakers guard, is accused of assaulting an 18-year-old woman who was working as a concierge at a Colorado resort where he was staying in June 2003.[1] Bryant, who is married, has admitted to having sexual intercourse with the woman but claims it was consensual; his accuser says he gripped her by the neck and forced her to have sex despite her protests. In October [2003], Eagle County Judge Frederick Gannett ordered Bryant to stand trial even while noting that the evidence presented by the prosecution was weak.

The Feminist Reaction

The defense tactics have been widely assailed by feminists, victim advocates, and other commentators as a sleazy exercise in victim trashing—particularly after an October 10 open court hearing in which lead Bryant attorney Pamela Mackey repeatedly mentioned the alleged victim's name despite the judge's ban on its public disclosure and suggested that the woman had had sexual relations with several other men in the days before her encounter with Bryant.

A typical reaction came from Cynthia Stone, an activist with the Colorado Coalition Against Sexual Assault: "Trying

1. The criminal rape case was dropped on September 1, 2004. The civil case against Bryant was settled on March 1, 2005.

to shift the blame is a standard tactic for rape defendants, but this was a new low in attacking the victim." Earlier, the defense team had come under fire for trying to obtain the young woman's mental health records. (Colorado laws will probably prevent them from doing so.)

Tying the Defendant's Hands

The spectacle of a young woman coming forward to bring rape charges against a wealthy, powerful man and being smeared with what feminist legal theorist Susan Estrich once dubbed a "nuts and sluts" defense is disturbing on a visceral level, and not just to feminists. But if Bryant is innocent—which is a presumption accorded to him in a court of law, and which in this case may well be true—it should be equally disturbing to think that a man accused of a despicable crime, one that potentially carries a sentence of life in prison, could have his hands tied when he tries to defend himself.

Take the issue of the complainant's therapy records—something that former Colorado prosecutor Amy Hitch, who successfully argued for excluding such evidence before the Colorado Court of Appeals, says should be brought into a rape case only if the prosecution makes an issue of it first. The desire to protect a victim's privacy is more than understandable, particularly in a sexual assault case. But what if a woman who says she was raped has a history of mental instability that could be relevant to the credibility of her accusations?

In 1991 similar issues were raised in a Maryland case involving charges of rape against a realtor named Gary Hart (no relation to the politician). His accuser, a 34-year-old cocktail waitress, claimed that they had been dating platonically and that she was staying at his house overnight when he brutally attacked her (although there was no evidence of the struggle she described). According to Hart, they had been sexually in-

Unappealing Alternatives

[Rape shield laws], this well-intentioned reform in our rape laws, has led to two unappealing alternatives: Either the defendant's legal presumption of innocence is flipped on its head, since rape shield laws unambiguously deny him access to potentially exculpatory evidence, or—as a practical matter—the woman's sexual history goes on trial regardless, permitting humiliating public scrutiny often likened to a second rape.

Dahlia Lithwick, New York Times, *August 8, 2004.*

volved and the woman got angry when he told her he was going on a trip without her.

Hart was acquitted after a controversial trial in which the defense stressed the woman's emotional instability, her tendency to react to rejection with sometimes violent rage, and her history of making fantastic claims of sexual assault to police and to psychiatrists.

The relevance of this evidence seems obvious. Yet prosecutors and victim advocates reacted as if the woman had been subjected to a gratuitous, vicious character attack. A letter in the *Baltimore Sun* complained that even if the alleged victim was not raped, she suffered "a brutal form of abuse . . . inside the courtroom." Yet if Hart was actually innocent, he was subjected to far worse abuse. Not only was he put on trial, but his name, unlike that of his accuser, was all over the papers; the negative publicity forced him to sell his business.

Questionable Claims

Hart, at least, was acquitted. In the same year, James Everett of Liggett, Washington, was convicted of raping a woman he had met through a dating service. He spent a year in prison before her story fell apart—partly because she reported an eerily similar man from the same dating service (who was exonerated) but also because Liggett was able to hire a private detective who found out that she had a history of mentally unstable behavior, including dubious claims of rape.

In Oregon, James Anderson was accused in 1989 of raping a fellow patient at a substance abuse clinic. He subsequently served a prison term. Anderson may or may not have been innocent, as he claims; but the case against him was based solely on the woman's testimony, and her serious credibility problems were kept out of the courtroom by the judge's application of the rape shield law.

While the prosecution said the woman failed to tell clinic staffers about the alleged rape because she was reluctant to discuss such "intimate details" with them, the suppressed records showed that the day before the incident, she had talked to the same counselors about an earlier rape and sexual abuse by her brother. Moreover, she had given several different and contradictory accounts of her supposed earlier victimization.

Suppressing Relevant Evidence

Courts in Iowa, Pennsylvania, Washington, and other states have ruled that evidence of an earlier false or dubious rape complaint by the accuser can be suppressed in a rape trial— even if it is relevant to the question of the defendant's guilt or innocence.

Even excluding all evidence of the woman's past sexual activity may not be the cut-and-dried issue it seems at first glance. In the Kobe Bryant case, for instance, the defense attorney's much-criticized claim that Bryant's accuser had very recently had sexual relations with two other men appears to have been corroborated by physical evidence.

Obviously, this does not mean (as the courts often assumed in the bad old days) that she must have been willing to have sex with Bryant as well, or that she was "asking for it." But it could provide an alternate explanation for the trauma to the woman's genitals found by the medical exam. Thus, in fairness to the defendant, it should be admissible.

Ironically, as Estrich noted in 1991, the greater willingness of prosecutors to pursue sexual assault cases in which the use of force is minimal and there is little corroborating evidence of injury makes the issue of the woman's credibility much more important, and thus gives the defense a greater incentive for attacks on her character. The courts have to walk a fine line between allowing complainants to be smeared and preventing defendants from fully confronting the witnesses against them.

For some feminists, of course, there is only one side to this issue. After the 1997 trial of sportscaster Marv Albert, defending the judge's decision to admit compromising information about Albert's sexual past but not about his accuser's, feminist attorney Gloria Allred decried "the notion that there's some sort of moral equivalency between the defendant and the victim."

Yet as long as the defendant hasn't been convicted, he and the alleged victim are indeed moral equals in the eyes of the law.

"[A] tracking device ... will alert authorities if a convicted sex offender is ... near a school or any other prohibited area."

Tracking Convicted Sexual Predators Will Protect Children

AnneMarie Knepper

Tracking convicted pedophiles is necessary to help law enforcement protect children from these predators, asserts AnneMarie Knepper in the following viewpoint. The claim that wearing a tracking device is inhumane is a weak argument when one considers the inhumanity of the crimes that hardcore sex offenders have committed, Knepper argues. These devices will prevent sexual crimes against children and will reduce the number of repeat offenders, she reasons. Knepper was, at the time of this writing, a columnist with the Daily Emerald, *the University of Oregon's independent student newspaper.*

As you read, consider the following questions:

1. According to Knepper, what events led to the passing of the Jessica Lunsford Act in Florida?

AnneMarie Knepper, "Florida Wins the Right Fight," *Daily Emerald* (Eugene, OR), May 5, 2005. www.dailyemerald.com. Reproduced by permission.

2. How does Florida's Jessica's Law add to offender registration requirements, in the author's view?

3. In the author's opinion, why does rehabilitation not work for the sex offenders that Jessica's Law targets?

Florida is a haven for strangeness, especially in terms of criminal behavior. Florida thieves once stole the remains of a relative because they believed the powdery substance [they] found in a tackle box was cocaine. In 1994, at a hotel near Miami Airport, the dead body of a 24-year-old woman was found underneath a bed, after the room's guests complained of a foul smell. Later that year in Fort Lauderdale, a hotel staff member discovered another dead body, this time of a 47-year-old man under a bed. Weird.

A Florida woman making meth accidentally dialed 911 instead of area code 921, hung up, and inadvertently led police directly to her well-stocked drug lab.

Then there is the whole voting in a democracy thing Floridians can't seem to get a handle on. Maybe it is the heat, or as I'm told, the humidity, that makes people crazy. Maybe it's the close proximity to other countries in case one needs to flee. Either way, wide-ranging media figures, from Adam Corolla of *Loveline* to the CBS News: *60 Minutes* anchors, have taken note: If something is so criminally strange or politically far-fetched it seems unbelievable, it probably happened in Florida.

Doing Something Right

Now this land of gator farms, Epcot Center and hanging chads has gone and done something—right? [In May 2005] Florida Gov. Jeb Bush signed the Jessica Lunsford Act into law. Jessica was 9 years old when she was abducted, sexually assaulted, then murdered by a convicted sex offender in March [2005]. John Evander Couey confessed to the crime and showed police where he buried her alive.

A New Way to Protect Children

In an ideal world, sex offenders would be completely reha-
bilitated when they get released from prison. But in reality,
these criminals have a particularly high rate of repeat offenses. Requiring a select few who are especially likely to
commit a sex crime again to wear GPS [Global Positioning
System] tracking devices would enable police to protect
children . . . in a way that simple registries cannot.

Boston University Daily Free Press, *April 15, 2004.*

The Jessica Lunsford bill was swiftly drafted and moved to
law unanimously after much emotional campaigning by the
girl's father, Mark Lunsford, and many Florida politicians. A
registered sexual predator confessed and was charged with the
death of another Florida girl, 13-year-old Sarah Lunde, only
weeks after Jessica's murder. The events enraged the citizens
and politicians of Florida and sped the legislative process for
what is now known as Jessica's Law.

The new law is the toughest in the nation, imposing a
mandatory sentence of 25 years to life in prison for people
convicted of sex crimes against children under 12 and requiring convicted sex offenders to wear global tracking devices on
their ankles for the rest of their lives.

The tracking device, which uses the satellite Global Positioning System, will alert authorities if a convicted sex offender is violating parole by being near a school or any other
prohibited area. It took Florida authorities nearly a month to
find Couey; if he had been wearing the tracking device, he
would have been found instantly.

Local police can monitor the global tracking devices any
time of day; makers of the device hope it will aid in the cre-

ation of a national database for sex offenders. Offenders who molest older children, 12 and older, will be required to wear the tracking device only during probation. It will be removed upon completion of their disciplinary program. This means Jessica's Law only affects pedophiles (adults who are sexually attracted to children), not, for example, a 19-year-old convicted of statutory rape for having sex with a 16-year-old.

Jessica's Law also strengthens and adds to offender registration requirements and makes it a felony to harbor a sexual offender. It is rumored that the people living with Couey in the trailer, where he says he held Jessica captive for days before killing her, were aware they were living with a sex offender who was unregistered in the area.

Critics argue the law is too expansive and doesn't allow for possible rehabilitation of sex offenders. Others say the global tracking device violates the offender's right to privacy—that tracking sex offenders like animals violates their humanity.

I say when you rape a young child, you have given up all rights to be treated as anything more than the animal you are. And rehabilitation? It doesn't work, not for the sex offenders this law targets. People who engage in sexual contact with 11-year-old children and younger have something fundamentally wrong with their brains. They have an incurable illness that can only be contained with constant work and attention through therapy, criminal analysis and an absence of vulnerable children in their presence. This is a near-impossible task to accomplish for the offenders as well as the judicial system.

With Jessica's Law, Florida hopes to stop child molestation before it starts. Lawmakers there claim the stiff penalties, which [went] into effect Sept. 1, [2005], will deter potential molesters from acting in the first place. Politicians are confident it will lower the numbers of repeat offenders. Jessica's Law will eliminate the issue of offenders "disappearing" when they change residence.

This is the first and likely only time I am going to say it, but it looks as though all states could take a lesson from Florida law. Gator country is really on to something with this one.

> *"Eyes in the sky are a great tool. . . . But when it comes to child sexual abusers, meaningful surveillance and community safety requires eyes on the ground."*

Tracking Convicted Sex Predators Will Not Protect Children

Kim Talman

Sex offender registries and tracking of sexual predators are no substitute for actual surveillance and supervision, claims Kim Talman in the following viewpoint. These tracking methods have become the equivalent of getting tough on child sexual abuse, she maintains. While registries appease public fear and make for good media sound bites, simply telling people about sex offenders in their neighborhood does not protect the public, Talman argues. Tracking cannot take the place of prison, probation, and parole, she asserts. Talman is a national advisory board member of the National Association to Protect Children (PROTECT).

Kim Talman, "Testimony of Kim Talman, New York Chair, National Association to Protect Children (PROTECT), before the New York Senate, Standing Committee on Crime Victims, Crime and Correction: Public Hearings on Megan's Law," June 7, 2005. Reproduced by permission of the author.

As you read, consider the following questions:

1. In Talman's opinion, what is the good news about the increasing distribution of information about convicted sex offenders?

2. How did the purpose of offender registries change in one decade, according to the author?

3. In the author's view, what are some meaningful ways that communities can safeguard children against sexual abusers?

Since the mid 1990s the purpose and goals of sex offender databases and registries has changed a great deal.

The History of Registries

Before "Megan's Law" and the Jacob Wetterling Act, there was the National Child Protection Act of 1993, also known as the "Oprah bill." This legislation was conceived by one of PROTECT's [National Association to Protect Children] founders, attorney Andrew Vachss, and promoted by television host Oprah Winfrey. It required the states to report criminal indictments and convictions to a federal database, enabling agencies that serve children all across America to have access to national background checks for the first time. While not creating a registry, per se, this Act was an extremely important first step towards protecting children by ensuring that authorities know who potentially dangerous predators are. The fundamental goal of this legislation was a first order of business: getting information about sex offenders into the hands of those with an immediate need for it, where it could be used in a measurable way to protect children.

The murder of 11-year-old Jacob Wetterling inspired the Jacob Wetterling Act a year later. This legislation required the states to establish sex offender registries. While public distribution of this information was permitted, it was not required.

The primary goal of the Wetterling Act was getting information about sex offenders into the hands of state and local law enforcement.

The murder of 7-year-old Megan Kanka led to the enactment of "Megan's Law" in 1996, which told states to open up their registries—at least in part—to the public. Americans were beginning to realize that there was information on these registries they had a powerful reason to know, and they wanted access. The goal of "Megan's Law," therefore was getting information about sex offenders into the hands of parents, caregivers, families and communities.

In one way, the increasing distribution of information about convicted sex offenders has had a profound impact on our nation. For the first time in American history, the ugly truth about the rampant sexual abuse of children is nearly impossible to sweep under the rug.

With each passing year from the mid-90's on, the number of convicted sex offenders showing up on public registries has steadily mushroomed. Nine years after "Megan's Law" was passed, there are over half a million registered sex offenders in the U.S. Millions of Americans have now had the unforgettable experience of logging on to the internet to find that sexual offenders are close to home—in fact, all around us. And many of us want greater protection for children as a result.

That's the good news.

The Bad News

The bad news—to put it bluntly—is that while sex offender registries are cheap, easy, popular and always good for media coverage, they are not—*even by the most widely optimistic standards*—any kind of substitute for real surveillance, supervision or public safety.

Mass Hysteria or Political Expediency?

Pedophilles and sex offenders can be very dangerous people. They can also get people elected, sell newspapers or get people to tune into the radio or television. . . .

Child sexual exploitation has now moved to the forefront of the national crime fighting agenda. . . .

The hope is that future or ongoing efforts to deal with sex offenders are grounded in verifiable initiatives to protect the public.

No one wants a dangerous convicted sex offender living in their neighborhood. However, the public should demand laws that are well intended and protect our families, not win elections or boost ratings.

Matthew T. Mangino,
Pennsylvania Law Weekly, *November 13, 2006.*

Please do not misunderstand. PROTECT . . . believes in sex offender registries. We want parents, grandparents, caregivers and other concerned citizens to have access to them. . . .

But in the decade since the passage of "Megan's Law," a very unfortunate thing has happened. Television's obsession with stranger abductions of children—which are a very tiny percentage of all sex crimes against children—fueled the public's fear of child sexual predators. And at the same time, the media began giving a great deal of coverage to sex offender registries, because they hit close to home for the public and are a treasure trove of two things the news media craves: pictures and real life stories.

An Inadequate Public Policy

Unfortunately, where the media goes, public policy makers are not far behind.

So, within one decade, what began as an effort to put useful information into the hands of child caregivers, law enforcement and communities became our foremost national policy for dealing with child sexual abusers:

- Registering as a sex offender became an actual sentence in and of itself!—one often justifying little or no prison time.

- Tougher registration requirements—enacted through perennial "get tough" sex offender bills—became the equivalent of getting tougher on child sexual abuse.

- Giving an unsuspecting public a "heads up!" about a child sexual predator in their neighborhood somehow became a substitute for actually protecting that public.

We should be clear about what we have been telling the public these last nine years about "Megan's Law." The message is: Child molesters on the registry are being watched. You and your family are safer because of it.

No Substitute for Surveillance

Now, with the horrible abduction and murder of little Jessica Lunsford of Florida by a repeat offender named John Couey, we are in danger of departing even further from reality. Whereas first we sought to give the public information about who is a danger and where they are—and then we began purporting that registration in and of itself made communities safer—now we see new federal legislation proposed that goes one step further: sex offender registries are now talked about as ways to "track" and "monitor" sex offenders, or actually conduct surveillance and impose restrictions.

The most dramatic, media-popular example of this is, of course, the GPS [Global Positioning System] satellite tracking device. This novel technology sounds so serious that it's hard for most Americans not to be impressed and a little excited.

Once again, the clear impression the public gets is that we will be all over these guys! Or as Representative Mark Foley said when he recently introduced legislation with Senator Orrin Hatch: we "will make prey of predators."

But it just doesn't work that way. Sex offender registries are sex offender registries. They are not a substitute for prison, probation or parole. Eyes in the sky are a great tool for law enforcement. But when it comes to child sexual abusers, meaningful surveillance and community safety requires eyes on the ground. . . .

Meaningful Safeguards

We want individuals who are known by their conduct to be sexually dangerous to children to be removed from society for as long as possible. Then, if and when they are released, we want them contained and under close surveillance for a very long time. Most . . . would agree there are no higher priorities than this.

Let me give you just six examples of meaningful community safeguards against child sexual abusers:

- Prohibit them from living with children.

- Conduct checks on activities and employment where children might be involved.

- Conduct unannounced visits and searches.

- Require mandatory sex offender treatment, whether it works or not.

- Search hard drives for child pornography.

- Have the ability to take law enforcement action if violations are found.

If you tell someone like me, a mother and hardware store owner from Long Island, that a known child molester is being released to my neighborhood, these are the types of protections that I hope you have in mind.

But not one of these things is possible through a sex offender registry program.

In order for the state to have the legal authority to do any of these things, a sex offender must be serving a sentence of probation or parole. Most offenders are on probation or parole a very short period of time, and most registered sex offenders are simply unsupervised. That's the dirty little secret that the public and media don't realize.

But I can assure you . . . , I am not that interested in the next John Couey moving in across the street from me with a GPS device on his leg and no supervision or restrictions whatsoever. I would take very little comfort in that, even if I did have the privilege of looking him up on the internet.

Containment and Surveillance

There will be some who will argue, "Fine. But probation and parole is a separate issue, and we are here to discuss the sex offender registry." The fact is, the sex offender registration and real community supervision have been blurred in the minds of the media, public and most lawmakers. This is primarily the result of policymakers and legislators representing *sex offender registration* as *sex offender management*. It would be a great disservice to compound this problem at a time when the public is desperately seeking assurance from its leaders that they will be protected from released sex offenders. If leaders respond to tragedies resulting from the lack of close surveillance and management of sex offenders—such as the Jessica Lunsford case in Florida—by calling for tougher sex offender registry requirements, then it is incumbent upon them to also take up the real solution: *containment and surveillance*. . . .

New reports are getting more frequent each month about local communities struggling desperately to cope with sex offenders in their midst. Municipal governments are attempting to zone sex offenders right out of town. Individual citizens are posting fliers and notifying neighbors. Offenders have been ordered to put signs in their yards.

None of these things should be happening. They are occurring because our laws and our criminal justice system are not taking the problem of sexual predators seriously. If and when convicted child sexual abusers are released from prison, they should be released to long-term probation or parole, under the close supervision of specialized sex offender teams.

That takes money and resources. Whether and how well we do it is the measure of our commitment to protecting children and safeguarding ... families.

Periodical Bibliography

The following articles have been selected to supplement the diverse views presented in this chapter.

Peter Aldhous — "Sex Offenders: Throwing Away the Key," *New Scientist*, February 21, 2007.

Beatrix Campbell — "Criminal Justice; Rape: The Truth," *New Statesman*, April 16, 2007.

Bruce K. Dixon — "State Laws Deficient in Dealing with Predators," *Clinical Psychiatry News*, January 2007.

T.R. Goldman — "Sex Crimes and Punishment," *New Jersey Law Journal*, May 29, 2006.

Alan Greenblatt — "Sex Offenders," *CQ Researcher*, September 8, 2006.

Richard B. Krueger — "The New American Witch Hunt," *Los Angeles Times*, March 11, 2007.

Jeninne Lee-St. John — "A Time Limit on Rape," *Time*, February 12, 2007.

Matthew T. Mangino — "Sex Offender Legislation: Mass Hysteria or Political Expediency?" *Pennsylvania Law Weekly*, November 13, 2006.

New York Times — "Wrong Turn on Sex Offenders," March 13, 2007.

Corey Rayburn — "To Catch a Sex Thief: The Burden of Performance in Rape and Sexual Assault Trials," *Columbia Journal of Gender and Law*, Summer 2006.

Jacob Sullum — "Fry 'Em? Even Sex Offenders Can Be Punished Too Severely," *Townhall.com*, March 7, 2007.

Terri Lynn Tersak — "VAWA Fails to Protect Women Who Need Protection the Most," Feminists.com, October 11, 2006. www.feminists.com.

For Further Discussion

Chapter 1

1. David A. Fahrenthold claims that the number of rapes in the United States has been decreasing since the 1970s. The National Institute of Justice maintains, however, that studies on rape rates can be misleading as rape definitions vary and many victims are unwilling to report rape. Do you think reduced rape rates reflect a change in how men and women view the rules of sexual consent or are they a statistical anomaly? Explain, citing evidence from the viewpoints.

2. Alberto R. Gonzales believes that Internet sexual predators are a serious and widespread problem. Benjamin Radford disputes this claim. What rhetorical strategies does each author use to support his argument? Which strategy do you find more persuasive? Citing from the viewpoints, explain your answers.

3. Wendy McElroy argues that false reports of rape hurt the real victims of rape. Cathleen Wilson does not dispute this claim but asserts that false reports are uncommon. The authors cite different types of evidence to support their claims. Is one form of evidence more persuasive? Explain why or why not, citing from the viewpoints.

Chapter 2

1. The chapter authors debate the significance of several causes of sexual violence. Which cause, if any, do you think contributes most to the problem of sexual violence? Citing from the viewpoints, explain.

2. What commonalities among the viewpoints on both sides of the debate can you find in this chapter? Explain, citing from the viewpoints.

3. Daniel Weiss maintains that pornography plays a significant role in sexual violence. Steve Chapman argues that if sexual violence is on the decline and pornography is more available, pornography may therefore reduce sexual violence. Which viewpoint do you find more persuasive? Explain.

4. According to Naomi Schaefer Riley, feminist messages encourage women to engage in behavior that puts them at risk of rape. Jennifer L. Pozner counters that such claims assume that rape is inevitable and nothing can be done to prevent it. What rhetorical strategies do the authors use to support their claims? Is one strategy more effective? Explain your reasoning, citing from the viewpoints.

Chapter 3

1. Laura Pedro argues that blaming the victim does not prevent rape and promotes dependence on men. Ron Liddle claims that avoiding rape is like avoiding other crimes—potential victims must assess the risks and accept responsibility for their decisions. What similarities can be found between Pedro's and Liddle's viewpoints and some of the viewpoints in the previous chapters? Which perspective do you find more persuasive? Citing from the viewpoints, explain.

2. Erin Varner asserts that hospitals should be required to advise rape victims of the availability of emergency contraception. Matt Sande disagrees, arguing that life begins at conception and that emergency contraception is therefore unethical abortion. The authors cite different types of evidence to support their claims. Do you find one form of evidence more persuasive? Explain why or why not, citing from the viewpoints.

3. Which of the viewpoints in the chapter focus on the behavior of the victims of sexual violence and which focus on the behavior of perpetrators? Which societal focus do

you think is the most effective way to respond to sexual violence? Citing from the viewpoints, explain your answer.

Chapter 4

1. Alberto R. Gonzales asserts that strict sex offender laws are necessary to reduce sexual violence. The editors of *America* argue, on the other hand, that such laws are ineffective and counterproductive. What evidence do the authors provide to support their claims? Which evidence do you find more persuasive? Explain.

2. Gloria Allred and Margery Somers maintain that rape shield laws are necessary to encourage women to report rape without fear. Cathy Young contends that many laws that protect victims make it hard for those falsely accused of rape to defend themselves. Whom do you think is in most need of protection, victims or perpetrators? Explain, citing from the viewpoints.

3. AnneMarie Knepper claims that tracking sexual predators will reduce repeat offenses. Kim Talman counters that tracking will not protect children and is a waste of resources. How does the rhetoric of each author differ? Which rhetorical strategy do you find more persuasive? Explain.

4. What commonalities can you find among the views on both sides of the sexual violence policy debates in this chapter? Citing from the viewpoints, explain your answer.

Organizations to Contact

The editors have compiled the following list of organizations concerned with the issues debated in this book. The descriptions are derived from materials provided by the organizations. All have publications or information available for interested readers. The list was compiled on the date of publication of the present volume; the information provided here may change. Readers need to remember that many organizations take several weeks or longer to respond to inquiries.

ACT for Kids
7 S. Howard St., Suite 200, Spokane, WA   99201-3816
toll-free: (866) 348-5437 • fax: (509) 747-0609
e-mail: resources@actforkids.org
Web site: www.actforkids.org

ACT for Kids is a nonprofit organization that provides resources, consultation, research, and training for the prevention and treatment of child abuse and sexual violence. The organization publishes workbooks, manuals, and books such as *He Told Me Not to Tell* and *How to Survive the Sexual Abuse of Your Child*.

American Coalition for Fathers and Children (ACFC)
1718 M St. NW, Suite 187, Washington, DC   20036
toll-free: (800) 978-3237 • fax: (703) 442-5313
e-mail: info@acfc.org
Web site: www.acfc.org

ACFC supports efforts to create a family law system that promotes equal rights for all parties affected by divorce and the breakup of a family. The coalition believes that the Violence Against Women Act destroys families and funds an antimale, profeminist ideological agenda. ACFC publishes the quarterly newspaper, the *Liberator*, articles from which are available on its Web site.

American Academy of Child and Adolescent Psychiatry (AACAP)
3615 Wisconsin Ave. NW, Washington, DC   20016-3007
(202) 966-7300 • fax: (202) 966-2891
Web site: www.aacap.org

AACAP is a nonprofit organization that supports and advances child and adolescent psychiatry through research and information distribution. The academy's goal is to provide information that will remove the stigma associated with mental illness and assure proper treatment for children who suffer from mental or behavioral disorders due to child abuse, molestation, or other factors. AACAP publishes the Facts for Families series on a variety of issues concerning disorders that may affect children and adolescents.

Association for the Rights of Catholics in the Church (ARCC)
PO Box 85, Southampton, MA   01073
(413) 527-9929 • fax: (413) 527-5877
e-mail: arccangel@charter.net
Web site: http://arcc-catholic-rights.org

Founded in 1980 by lay and clerical Catholics, ARCC's primary goal is to promote accountability, institutionalize shared decision making, and preserve the rights of all Catholics. On its Web site, ARCC provides access to archives of its newsletter, the *ARCC Light*, and documents written by ARCC members, including "Vatican Must Deal Openly with Priest Pedophilia Cases."

Association for the Treatment of Sexual Abuse (ATSA)
4900 SW Griffith Dr., Suite 274, Beaverton, OR   97005
(503) 643-1023 • fax: (503) 643-5084
e-mail: igrid@atsa.com
Web site: www.atsa.com

To eliminate sexual victimization and protect communities from sex offenders, ATSA fosters research, furthers professional education, and advances professional standards and practices in the field of sex offender evaluation and treatment. The association publishes the quarterly *ATSA Journal*. The ATSA Web site features links to other organizations and access to current research and conferences.

Faith Trust Institute
2400 N. Forty-fifth St., Suite 101, Seattle, WA   98103
(206) 634-1903 • fax: (206) 634-0115
e-mail: info@faithtrustinstitute.org
Web site: http://faithtrustinstitute.org

The institute serves as an interreligious educational resource addressing issues of sexual and domestic violence. The goal of the institute is to help religious leaders end abuse. It publishes books and videos on sexual abuse by clergy, the quarterly *Journal of Religion and Abuse*, and the quarterly newsletter *Working Together*, which includes articles, editorials, book reviews, resources, and information about local, national, and international prevention efforts. Recent issues of the newsletter are available on its Web site.

Generation Five
3288 Twenty-first St. #171, San Francisco, CA   94110
(510) 251-8552 • fax: (510) 251-8566
e-mail: info@generationfive.org
Web site: www.generationfive.org

The mission of Generation Five is to end the sexual abuse of children within five generations. Through survivor leadership, community organization, and public action, Generation Five works to interrupt and mend the intergenerational impact of child sexual abuse on individuals, families, and communities. Generation Five integrates child sexual abuse prevention into social movements targeting family violence, economic oppression, and gender and cultural discrimination. It also collaborates with other organizations to ensure that accessible, culturally relevant services are available to both survivors of child sexual assault and offenders.

Interfaith Sexual Trauma Institute (ISTI)
Saint John's Abbey and University, Collegeville, MN   56321
e-mail: isti@csbsju.edu
Web site: www.csbsju.edu/isti

To facilitate safe, healthy, and trustworthy communities of faith, ISTI promotes the prevention of sexual abuse, exploitation, and harassment through research, education, and publication. The institute facilitates healing for survivors, communities of faith, and offenders. ISTI publishes books, including *Before the Fall: Preventing Pastoral Sexual Abuse* and *Recovering the Lost Self: Shame Healing for Victims of Clergy Sexual Abuse* as well as the *ISTI Sun* newsletter, which includes articles such as "Abuse of Power, Part I and II," available on its Web site.

Male Survivor
5505 Connecticut Ave. NW, Washington, DC   20015-2601
toll-free: (800) 738-4181
Web site: www.malesurvivor.org

Male Survivor, formerly National Organization on Male Sexual Victimization (NOMSV), believes that sexually victimized boys and men need added support to come forward and ask for help. Identification, assessment, and intervention help prevent abused boys from becoming self-destructive or abusive adolescents and men. The organization, which respects the diversity of sexual abuse survivors, serves anyone who has been sexually abused. Male Survivor helps the public and the media to recognize and understand males who have been sexually abused and promotes action to confront and fight male sexual abuse. The Male Survivor Web site provides information for survivors, clinicians, and caregivers. It also provides access to news and *Male Survivor*, its quarterly newsletter.

Men Can Stop Rape
PO Box 57144, Washington, DC   20037
(202) 265-6530 • fax: (202) 265-4362

e-mail: info@mencanstoprape.org
Web site: www.mencanstoprape.org

Men Can Stop Rape mobilizes male youth to prevent men's violence against women. Their mission is to build young men's capacity to challenge harmful aspects of traditional masculinity, to value alternative visions of male strength, and to embrace their vital role as allies with women and girls in fostering healthy relationships and gender equality. Articles, the cartoon strip "The Saga of Anti-Rape Man," and the periodic column, ". . .She Said," are available on its Web site.

Miles Foundation

PO Box 423, Newtown, CT   06470-0423
(203) 270-7861
e-mail: milesfdn@aol.com or milesfd@yahoo.com
Web site: http://hometown.aol.com/milesfdn

The Miles Foundation is a private, nonprofit organization providing comprehensive services to victims of violence, including sexual violence, associated with the military. The foundation furnishes professional education and training to civilian community-based service providers and military personnel, conducts research, and serves as a resource center for policy makers, advocates, journalists, scholars, researchers, and students. It also fosters administrative and legislative initiatives to improve the military response to domestic and sexual violence. A list of publications and resources can be found on its Web site.

National Center for Missing and Exploited Children (NCMEC)

699 Prince St., Alexandria, VA   22314
toll-free: (800) THE-LOST
Web site: www.missingkids.com

The NCMEC serves as a clearinghouse of information on missing and exploited children and coordinates child protection efforts with the private sector. A number of publications on these issues are available, including guidelines for parents whose children are testifying in court, help for abused children, and booklets such as *Child Molesters: A Behavioral Analysis* and *How to Keep Your Child Safe: A Message to Every Parent.*

National Coalition Against Domestic Violence (NCADV)
1633 Q St. NW, Suite 210, Washington, DC   20009
(202) 745-121
Web site: www.ncadv.org

NCADV believes that violence against women and children results from the use of force or threat to achieve and maintain control over others in intimate relationships, including sexual violence. The coalition believes that the abuses of power in society foster battering by perpetuating conditions that condone violence against women and children. NCADV therefore works to change these societal conditions. The coalition publishes fact sheets and a suggested reading list, which are available on its Web site. Its newsletters, the *Grassroots Connection*, and the *Voice: A Journal of the Battered Women's Movement* are available with membership.

National Criminal Justice Reference Service (NCJRS)
PO Box 6000, Rockville, MD   20849-6000
(301) 519-5500 • fax: (301) 519-5212
e-mail: askncjrs@ncjrs.org
Web site: www.ncjrs.org

NCJRS is an agency of the U.S. Department of Justice established to prevent and reduce crime and to improve the criminal justice system. The NCJRS Web site provides access to numerous reports on crime and justice, including *The Culture of Prison Sexual Violence* and *Staying Safe: What You Can Do About Sexual Violence.*

National Sexual Violence Resource Center (NSVRC)
123 N. Enola Dr., Enola, PA   17025
toll-free: (877) 739-3895 • fax: (717)909-0714

e-mail: resources@nsvrc.org
Web site: www.nsvrc.org

The NSVRC, a project of the Pennsylvania Coalition Against Rape, is a comprehensive collection and distribution center for information, research and emerging policy on sexual violence intervention and prevention. In addition to tracking resources developed throughout the country, the NSVRC publishes a semiannual newsletter, issues press releases and talking points on current events, and coordinates an annual national sexual assault awareness month campaign in April.

One in Four, Inc.
PO Box 6912, Williamsburg, VA   23188-6912
(757) 221-2191 • fax: (757) 221-2988
e-mail: rvtour@oneinfourusa.org
Web site: www.oneinfourusa.org

The mission of One in Four, Inc., formerly NO MORE, National Organization of Men's Outreach for Rape Education, is to prevent rape through the thoughtful application of theory and research to rape prevention programming. One in Four, Inc. (the name refers to the statistical fact that one in four college women have survived rape or an attempted rape) provides educational tools for colleges, high schools, the military, and local community organizations. It also serves as an umbrella organization and support system for all-male sexual assault peer education groups who call themselves "One in Four."

The Safer Society Foundation
PO Box 340, Brandon, VT   05733-0340
(802) 247-3132 • fax: (802) 247-4233
Web site: www.safersociety.org

The Safer Society Foundation is a national research, advocacy, and referral center for the prevention of sexual abuse of children and adults. The Safer Society Press publishes studies and books on the prevention of sexual abuse and on treatment for sexual abuse victims and offenders, including *Back on Track: Boys Dealing with Sexual Abuse.*

Students Active For Ending Rape (SAFER)
25 Washington St., Suite 411, Brooklyn, NY   11201
(347) 689-3914
Web site: www.safercampus.org

SAFER provides training and support to college and university students so that they can win improvements to their schools' sexual assault prevention and response activities. By offering students the necessary support and resources, confidence building, and leadership training, SAFER empowers student activists to rally the community and push school administrations to take action.

Survivors Network of Those Abused by Priests (SNAP)
PO Box 641, Chicago, IL   60680
(312) 409-2720
Web site: www.survivorsnetwork.org

SNAP provides support for men and women who have been sexually abused by any clergy, including priests, brothers, nuns, deacons, and teachers. The network provides an extensive phone network, advocacy, information, and referrals. On its Web site, SNAP provides access to stories, statements, and speeches from survivors, a discussion board, news, and information on legal issues.

U.S. Department of Justice Office on Violence Against Women
800 K St. NW, Suite 920, Washington, DC   20530
(202) 307-6026 • fax: (202) 305-2589
Web site: www.ovw.usdoj.gov

The U.S Department of Justice Office of Violence Against Women (OVW) provides federal leadership to reduce violence against women, dating violence, sexual assault, and stalking. The office also administers Violence Against Women Act grants to state, local, tribal, and nonprofit entities that respond to violence against women. OVW publications on domestic violence and teen dating violence can be found at the National

Criminal Justice Reference Service Web site identified above. The OVW Web site publishes fact sheets on domestic violence and teen dating violence, the Violence Against Women Act, and related legislation such as the Violent Crime Control and Law Enforcement Act.

Voice of the Faithful (VOTF)
PO Box 423, Newton Upper Falls, MA   02464
(617) 558-5252 • fax: (617) 558-0034
Web site: www.votf.org

VOTF is a lay group formed in response to the 2002 clergy sexual abuse crisis with the aim of restoring trust between the Catholic laity and hierarchy and rebuilding the Catholic Church. The organization supports survivors and "priests of integrity" and promotes church reform that involves the laity in church governance. The VOTF Web site provides access to survivor and clergy support services and statements and articles on the child sexual abuse crisis.

Bibliography of Books

Emilie Buchwald, Pamela Fletcher, and Martha Roth, eds.
Transforming a Rape Culture. Minneapolis: Milkweed, 2004.

Shawna Cleary
Sex Offenders and Self-Control: Explaining Sexual Violence. New York: LFB Scholarly, 2004.

B.J. Cling, ed.
Sexualized Violence Against Women and Children: A Psychology and Law Perspective. New York: Guilford, 2004.

Carolyn E. Cocca
Jailbait: The Politics of Statutory Rape Laws in the United States. Albany: State University of New York Press, 2004.

Gregory M. Cooper and Michael R. King
Predators: Who They Are and How to Stop Them. Amherst, NY: Prometheus, 2007.

Duane L. Dobbert
Halting the Sexual Predators Among Us: Preventing Attack, Rape, and Lust Homicide. Westport, CT: Praeger, 2004.

Norman J. Finkel
Emotions and Culpability: How the Law Is at Odds with Psychology, Jurors, and Itself. Washington, DC: American Psychological Association, 2006.

Jake Goldenflame	*Overcoming Sexual Terrorism: 40 Ways to Protect Your Children from Sexual Predators.* Philadelphia: Xlibris, 2004.
Chris Greer	*Sex Crime and the Media: Sex Offending and the Press in a Divided Society.* Portland, OR: Willan, 2003.
Karen Heimer and Candace Kruttschnitt, eds.	*Gender and Crime: Patterns of Victimization and Offending.* New York: New York University Press, 2006.
James F. Hodgson and Debra S. Kelley, eds.	*Sexual Violence: Policies, Practices, and Challenges in the United States and Canada.* Westport, CT: Praeger, 2002.
Eric S. Janus	*Failure to Protect: America's Sexual Predator Laws and the Rise of the Preventive State.* Ithaca, NY: Cornell University Press, 2006.
Mark J. Kittleson et al.	*The Truth About Rape.* New York: Facts On File, 2005.
John Q. La Fond	*Preventing Sexual Violence: How Society Should Cope with Sex Offenders.* Washington, DC: American Psychological Association, 2005.
Martin L. Lalumiere et al.	*The Causes of Rape: Understanding Individual Differences in Male Propensity for Sexual Aggression.* Washington, DC: American Psychological Association, 2005.
Judith Levine	*Harmful to Minors: The Perils of Protecting Children from Sex.* New York: Thunder's Mouth, 2003.

Paul Nathanson and Katherine K. Young — *Legalizing Misandry: From Public Shame to Systemic Discrimination Against Men.* Montreal: McGill-Queen's University Press, 2006.

Laura L. O'Toole, Jessica R. Schiffman, and Margie L. Kiter Edwards, eds. — *Gender Violence: Interdisciplinary Perspectives.* New York: New York University Press, 2007.

Thomas G. Plante, ed. — *Sin Against the Innocents: Sexual Abuse by Priests and the Role of the Catholic Church.* Westport, CT: Praeger, 2004.

Frances P. Reddington and Betsy Wright Kreisel, eds. — *Sexual Assault: The Victims, the Perpetrators, and the Criminal Justice System.* Durham, NC: Carolina Academic Press, 2005.

Anna C. Salter — *Predators: Pedophiles, Rapists, and Other Sex Offenders: Who They Are, How They Operate, and How We Can Protect Ourselves and Our Children.* New York: Basic, 2003.

Kerry Sheldon and Dennis Howlitt — *Sex Offenders and the Internet.* Hoboken, NJ: Wiley, 2007.

Cheryl Brown Travis — *Evolution, Gender, and Rape.* Cambridge, MA: MIT Press, 2003.

Index